# PLAYS

## Pedro Calderón de la Barca

# PLAYS

# Pedro Calderón de la Barca

Selected by

Vladimir Orel

## Table of Contents

| | |
|---|---|
| THE WONDER WORKING MAGICIAN | 9 |
| LIFE IS A DREAM | 137 |
| THE PURGATORY OF ST. PATRICK | 221 |

### From the Editor

The son and one of the creators of the Spanish "Golden Age", Calderón (1600-1681) was an inexhaustible playwright — he wrote more than 200 original comedies and *autos sacramentales*, dramatic works in which he gave artistic expression to seemingly abstract concepts of theology. A persistent labourer, Calderón continued reshaping and rewriting his own work, seeking esthetic perfection. Tightly knit, his plays are full of intricately organized action and unexpected, yet natural, motivations.

# THE WONDER-WORKING MAGICIAN

## Translated by Denis Florence MacCarthy

### PERSONS

CYPRIAN.
THE DEMON.
LELIUS, The Governor of Antioch's Son.
FLORUS, friend of Lelius.
MOSCON, Servant of Cyprian.
CLARIN, Servant of Cyprian.
THE GOVERNOR OF ANTIOCH.
FABIUS, his Servant.
LYSANDER, the reputed Father of Justina.
JUSTINA.
LIVIA, her Maid.
A Servant.
A Soldier.
ATTENDANTS, Soldiers, People.

SCENE — Antioch and its environs.

### ACT THE FIRST.

### SCENE I.

### A WOOD NEAR ANTIOCH.

Enter CYPPRIAN in a Student's gown, followed by CLARIN and MOSCON, as poor Scholars, carrying books.

CYPRIAN. In the pleasant solitude
Of this tranquil spot, this thicket
Formed of interlacing boughs,
Buds, and flowers, and shrubs commingled,

You may leave me, leaving also,
As my best companions, with me,
(For I need none else) those books
Which I bad you to bring hither
From the house; for while, to-day,
Antioch, the mighty city,
Celebrates with such rejoicing
The great temple newly finished
Unto Jupiter, the bearing
Thither, also, of his image
Publicly, in grant procession,
To its shrine to be uplifted; —
I, escaping the confusion
Of the streets and squares, have flitted
Hitherward, to spend in study
What of daylight yet may glimmer.
Go, enjoy the festival,
Go to Antioch and mingle
In its various sports, returning
When the sun descending sinketh
To be buried in the waves,
Which, beneath the dark clouds' fringes,
Round the royal corse of gold,
Shine like sepulchres of silver.
Here you'll find me.

MOSCON. Sir, although
Most decidedly my wish is
To behold the sports, yet I
Cannot go without a whisper
Of some few five thousand words,
Which I'll give you in a jiffy.
Can it be that on a day
Of such free, such unrestricted
Revelry, and mirth, and fun,
You with your old books come hither

To this country place, rejecting
All the frolic of the city?

CLARIN. Well, I think my master's right;
For there's nothing more insipid
Than a grand procession day,
Half fandangos, priests, and fiddles.

MOSCON. Clarin, from the first to last,
All your life you've been a trickster,
A smart temporizing toady,
A bold flatterer, a trimmer,
Since you praise the thoughts of others,
And ne'er speak your own.

CLARIN. The civil
Way to tell a man he lies
Is to say he's wrong: — you twig me,
Now I think I speak my mind.

CYPRIAN. Moscon, Clarin, both I bid ye
Cease this silly altercation.
It is ever thus betwixt ye,
Puffed up with your little knowledge
Each maintains his own opinion.
Go, and (as I've said) here seek me
When night falls, and with the thickness
Of its shadows veils from view
This most fair and wondrous system
Of the universe.

MOSCON. How comes it,
That although you have admitted
'Tis not right to see the feast,
Yet you go to see it?

CLARIN. Simple
Is the answer: no one follows
The advice which he has given
To another.

MOSCON (aside). To see Livia,
Would the gods that I were winged.
(Exit.

CLARIN (aside). If the honest truth were told
Livia is the girl that gives me
Something worth the living for.
Even her very name has in it
This assurance: 'Livia', yes,
Minus 'a', I live for 'Livi'.
(Exit.

## SCENE II.

CYPRIAN. Now I am alone, and may,
If my mind can be so lifted,
Study the great problem which
Keeps my soul disturbed, bewilder'd,
Since I read in Pliny's page
The mysterious words there written.
Which define a god; because
It doth seem beyond the limits
Of my intellect to find
One who all these signs exhibits.
This mysterious hidden truth
Must I seek for.
(Reads.

## SCENE III.

Enter the DEMON, in gala dress. CYPRIAN.

DEMON (aside). Though thou givest
All thy thoughts to the research,
Cyprian, thou must ever miss it,
Since I'll hide it from thy mind.

CYPRIAN. There's a rustling in this thicket.
Who is there? who art thou?

DEMON. Sir,
A mere stranger, who has ridden
All this morning up and down
These dark groves, not knowing whither,
Having lost my way, my horse,
To the emerald that encircles,
With a tapestry of green,
These lone hills, I've loosed, it gives him
At the same time food and rest.
I'm to Antioch bound, on business
Of importance, my companions
I have parted from; through listless
Lapse of thought (a thing that happens
To the most of earthly pilgrims),
I have lost my way, and lost
Comrades, servants, and assistants.

CYPRIAN. I am much surprised to learn
That in view of the uplifted
Towers of Antioch, you thus
Lost your way. There's not a single
Path that on this mountain side,
More or less by feet imprinted,
But doth lead unto its walls,
As to its one central limit.
By whatever path you take,
You'll go right.

DEMON. It is an instance
Of that ignorance which in sight
Even of truth the true goal misses.
And as it appears not wise
Thus to enter a strange city
Unattended and unknown,
Asking even my way, 'tis fitter
That 'till night doth conquer day,
Here while light doth last, to linger;
By your dress and by these books
Round you, like a learned circle
Of wise friends, I see you are
A great student, and the instinct
Of my soul doth ever draw me
Unto men to books addicted.

CYPRIAN. Have you studied much?

DEMON. Well, no;
But I've knowledge quite sufficient
Not to be deemed ignorant.

CYPRIAN. Then, what sciences know you?

DEMON. Many.

CYPRIAN. Why, we cannot reach even one
After years of studious vigil,
And can you (what vanity!)
Without study know so many?

DEMON. Yes; for I am of a country
Where the most exalted science
Needs no study to be known.

CYPRIAN. Would I were a happy inmate
Of that country! Here our studies
Prove our ignorance more.

DEMON. No figment
Is the fact that without study,
I had the superb ambition
For the first Professor's chair
To compete, and thought to win it,
Having very numerous votes.
And although I failed, sufficient
Glory is it to have tried.
For not always to the winner
Is the fame. If this you doubt,
Name the subject of your study,
And then let us argue on it;
I not knowing your opinion,
Even although it be the right,
Shall the opposite view insist on.

CYPRIAN. I am greatly gratified
That you make this proposition.
Here in Plinius is a passage
Which much anxious thought doth give me
How to understand, to know
Who's the God of whom he has written.

DEMON. 'Tis that passage which declares
(Well I know the words) this dictum:
"God is one supremest good,
One pure essence, one existence,
Self-sustained, all sight, all hands."

CYPRIAN. Yes, 'tis true.

DEMON. And what is in it

So abstruse?

CYPRIAN. I cannot find
Such a god as Plinius figures.
If he be the highest good,
Then is Jupiter deficient
In that attribute; we see him
Acting like a mortal sinner
Many a time, — this, Danae,
This, Europa, too, doth witness.
Can then, by the Highest Good,
All whose actions, all whose instincts,
Should be sacred and divine,
Human frailty be committed?

DEMON. These are fables which the learned
First made use of, to exhibit
Underneath the names of gods
What in truth was but a hidden
System of philosophy.

CYPRIAN. This reply is not sufficient,
Since such awe is due to God,
None should dare to Him attribute,
None should stain His name with sins,
Though these sins should be fictitious.
And considering well the case,
If the highest good is figured
By the gods, of course, they must
Will what is the best and fittest;
How, then, can some gods wish one thing,
Some another? This we witness
In the dubious responses
Which are by their statues given.
Here you cannot say I speak of
Learned abstractions of the ideal.

To two armies, if two shrines
Promise give of being victors,
One, of course, must lose the battle:
The conclusion is so simple, —
Need I say it? that two wills,
Mutually antagonistic,
Cannot lead unto one end.
They being thus in opposition,
One we must consider good,
One as bad we must consider.
But an evil will in God
Would imply a contradiction:
Then the highest good can dwell not
Among gods who know division.

DEMON. I deny your major, since
These responses may be given,
By the oracles, for ends
Which our intellectual vision
Cannot reach: 'tis providence.
Thus more good may have arisen
To the loser in that battle
Than its gain could bring the winner.

CYPRIAN. Granted; but that god ought not,
For the gods are not malicious,
To have promised victory; —
It would have been quite sufficient,
Without this most false assurance,
The defeat to have permitted.
Then if God must be all sight,
Every god should see distinctly
With clear vision to the end;
Seeing THAT, he erred in fixing
On a false conclusion; then
Though the deity may with fitness

Be divided into persons,
Yet His essence must be single
In the smallest circumstance.

DEMON. It was needful for this business,
That the oracle should rouse
The two hosts alike.

CYPRIAN. If fitting,
There were genii that could rouse them
(Good and bad, as they're distinguished
By the learned), who are, in fact,
Spirits who among us mingle,
And who good and evil acts,
Evil thoughts, suggest and whisper,
A convincing argument
For the immortal soul's existence:
Of these ministers could God
Have made use, nor thus exhibit
He was capable of a lie
To effect his ends?

DEMON. Consider,
That these seeming contradictions
Cannot our firm faith diminish
In the oneness of the gods,
If in things of higher import
They know naught of dissonance.
Take man's wondrous frame, for instance,
Surely that majestic structure
Once conception doth exhibit.

CYPRIAN. If man's maker then were one
He some vantage must have given him
O'er the others; and if they
All are equal, — 'tis admitted

That they are so, from the fact
Of their mutual opposition
To each other, — when the thought
Of creating man was hinted
By one god, another could
Say, "No, no, I do not wish it."
Then if God must be all hands,
Time might come when they would differ,
One creating, one undoing,
Ere the other's work was finished,
Since the power of each was equal,
But unequal were their wishes.
Which of these two powers would conquer?

DEMON. On impossible and false issues
There can be no argument; —
But your premises admitting,
Say what then?

CYPRIAN. That there must be
One sole God, all hands, all vision,
Good Supreme, supreme in grace,
One who cannot err, omniscient,
One the highest, none can equal,
Not beginning, yet the Beginner,
One pure essence, one sole substance,
One wise worker, ozone sole willer; —
And though He in one or two
Or more persons be distinguished,
Yet the sovereign Deity
Must be one, sublime and single,
The first cause of every cause,
The first germ of all existence.

DEMON. How can I deny so clear,
(They rise.

So conclusive a position?

CYPRIAN. Do you feel it?

DEMON. Who would not
Feel to find another quicker
In the rivalry of wit? —
And though I am not deficient
In an answer, I restrain it,
Hearing steps approaching hither
Through the wood; besides 'tis time
I proceeded to the city.

CYPRIAN. Go in peace.

DEMON. Remain in peace. —
(Aside.
So involved in study IS he,
That I now must wean him from it,
Weaving round him the bewitchment
Of rare beauty. Since I have leave
To attempt my fires to kindle
In Justina's breast, one stroke,
Thus, two vengeances shall give me.
(Exit.

CYPRIAN. Never saw I such a man.
But since still my people linger,
I, the cause of so much doubt,
Will now strive to reconsider.
(He resumes his reading, without perceiving the approach of those who enter.

## SCENE IV.

Enter LELIUS and FLORUS. — CYPRIAN.

LELIUS. Further let us not proceed;
For these rocks, these boughs so thickly
Interwoven, that the sun
Cannot even find admittance,
Shall be the sole witnesses
Of our duel.

FLORUS. Then, this instant
Draw your sword; for here are deeds,
If in words elsewhere we've striven.

LELIUS. Yes, I know that in the field,
While the tongue is mute, the glitter
Of the sword speaks thus.
(They fight.

CYPRIAN. What's this?
Hold, good Florus! Lelius, listen! —
Here until your rage is calmed,
Even unarmed I stand betwixt ye.

LELIUS. Thus to interrupt my vengeance,
Whence, O Cyprian, have you risen
Like a spectre?

FLORUS. A wild wood-god,
Have you from these tree-trunks issued?

## SCENE V.

Enter MOSCON and CLARIN.

MOSCON. Yonder, where we left our master,
I hear sword-strokes; run, run quickly.

CLARIN. Well, except to run away,
I am anything but nimble; —
Truly a retiring person.

MOSCON and CLARIN. Sir . . . .

CYPRIAN. No more: your gabble irks me. —
How? What's this? Two noble friends,
Who in blood, in birth, in lineage,
Are to-day of Antioch all
Its expectancy, the city's
Eye of fashion, one the son
Of the Governor, of the princely
House Colalto, one the heir,
Thus to peril, as of little
Value, two such precious lives
To their country and their kindred?

LELIUS. Cyprian, although respect
Which on many grounds I give thee,
Holds my sword suspended thus
In due deference for an instant, —
To the scabbard's calm repose
It hath got no power to win it.
Thou of science knowest more,
Than the duel, pretermitting
This, that when two nobles meet
In the field, no power can link them
Friends again, save this, that one

Must his life give as a victim.

FLORUS. This I also say, and ask thee,
With thy people, that thou quittest,
Leaving us to end our quarrel
Without any help or hindrance.

CYPRIAN. Though it seems to you my calling
Makes me know the laws but little
Of the duel — that strict code
Valour and vain pride have written,
You are wrong, for I was born
With the obligations fitting
Rank like yours, to know in truth
Infamy and honour's limits.
The devotion to my studies
Has my courage not diminished,
For they oftentimes shake hands
Arms and letters as though kinsmen.
If to meet here in the field
Was the quarrel's first condition,
Having met and fought, its lies
Calumny can never whisper.
And the cause you thus can tell me
Of the feud that brings you hither;
For I promise, if, on hearing
What to me is thus committed,
I perceive that satisfaction
Must on either side be given,
Here to leave you both alone,
Unobserved by any witness.

LELIUS. Then on this condition solely,
That you leave us, when the bitter
Truth is told, to end our quarrel,
I to tell the cause am willing.

I a certain lady love,
The same lady as his mistress
Florus also loves; now see,
How incompatible are our wishes! —
Since betwixt two jealous nobles
No mediation is admitted.

FLORUS. I this lady love so much,
That the sunlight I would hinder
From beholding her sweet face.
Since then all interposition
Is in vain, pray stand aside,
And our quarrel let us finish.

CYPRIAN. Stay, for one more thing I'd know.
Tell me this of your fair mistress,
Is she possible to your hopes,
Or impossible to your wishes? —

LELIUS. Oh: she is so good and wise,
That if even the sun enkindled
Jealousy in the heart of Florus,
It was jealousy pure and simple,
Without cause, for even the sun
Dare not look upon her visage.

CYPRIAN. Would you marry with her, then?

FLORUS. This is all my heart's ambition.

CYPRIAN. And would you?

LELIUS. Ah, would to heaven,
I were destined for such blisses! —
For although she's very poor,
Virtue dowers her with its riches.

CYPRIAN. If you both aspire to wed her,
Is it not an act most wicked,
Most unworthy, thus beforehand
Her unspotted fame to injure?
What will say the world, if one
Of you two shall marry with her
After having killed the other
For her sake? The supposition
Is not probable in fact,
To imagine it is sufficient.
I by no means say you should
Each your chances try to win her
At one time, for I would blush
Such a craven proposition
Came from me, because the lover
Who could keep his jealousy hidden,
Would condone even shame thereafter,
Were the opportunity given;
But I say that you should learn
Which of you it is your mistress
Gives the preference to, then . . . .

LELIUS. Stay! —
For it were an act too timid,
Too faint-hearted thus to ask
Of a lady such admission
As the choosing him or me.
For if me she chose, more fixed
Is my call for satisfaction;
For his fault has this addition,
He loves one who loves but me.
If to him the choice is given,
This intensifies my anger
All the more, that she, my mistress,
Whom I love, should love another.

Her selection could do little
In the matter, which at last
To our swords should be committed, —
The accepted for his honour,
The refused for his dismissal.

FLORUS. I confess that I adopt
Altogether that opinion,
Still the privilege of selection
May to ladies be permitted;
So to-day I mean to ask her
Of her father. 'Tis sufficient
To have come here to the field,
And my naked sword uplifted,
(Specially as one is by
Who the further fight resisteth,)
For my honour; — so to sheathe,
Lelius, my sword I'm willing.
(Sheathes his sword.

LELIUS. By your argument and action,
Florus, you have half convinced me;
I forego the remaining half —
True or false, I thus act with you.
(Sheathes his sword.
I to-day will seek her father.

CYPRIAN. On, of course, the supposition,
That this lady you pay court to
Suffers naught by the admission,
Since you both have spoken proudly
Of her virtue and her strictness,
Tell me who she is; for I,
Who am held throughout the city
In esteem, would for you both
Speak to her at first a little

That she thus may be prepared
When her father tells your wishes.

LELIUS. You are right.

CYPRIAN. Her name?

FLORUS. Justina,
Daughter of Lysander.

CYPRIAN. Little,
Now that I have heard her name,
Seem the praises you have given her;
She is virtuous as she's noble.
Instantly I'll pay my visit.

FLORUS (aside). May heaven grant that in my favour
Her cold heart be moved to pity!
(Exit.

LELIUS. Love, my hopes with laurels crown
When they are to her submitted!
(Exit.

CYPRIAN. Further mischief or misfortune,
Grant me, heaven, that I may hinder!
(Exit.

## SCENE VI.

MOSCON, CLARIN.

MOSCON. Has your worship heard our master
Now is gone to pay a visit
To Justina?

CLARIN. Yes, my lord.
But what matter if he didn't?

MOSCON. Matter quite enough, your worship;
He has no business there.

CLARIN. Why, prithee?

MOSCON. Why? because I die for Livia,
Who is maid to this Justina,
And I wouldn't have even the sun
Get a glimpse of her through the window.

CLARIN. Well, that's good; but, for a lady,
To contend were worse than silly,
Whom I mean to make my wife.

MOSCON. Excellent, faith! the fancy tickles
Quite my fancy. Let her say
Who it is that annoys or nicks her
To a nicety. Let's go see her,
And she'll choose.

CLARIN. A good idea! —
Though I fear she'll pitch on you.

MOSCON. Have you then that wise suspicion?

CLARIN. Yes; for always these same Livias
Choose the worst, th'ungrateful minxes.
(Exeunt.

## SCENE VII.

A HALL IN THE HOUSE OF LYSANDER.

Enter JUSTINA and LYSANDER.

JUSTINA. Consolation, sir, is vain,
After what I've seen to-day:
The whole city, madly gay,
Error-blinded and insane,
Consecrating shrine and fane
To an image, which I know,
Cannot be a god, although
Some demoniac power may pass,
Making breathe the silent brass
As a proof that it is so.

LYSANDER. Fair Justina, thou indeed,
Wert not who thou art, if thou
Didst not weep as thou dost now,
Didst not in thy pure heart bleed
For what Christ's divinest creed
Suffers on this sinful day.

JUSTINA. Thus my lineage I display: —
For thy child I could not be,
Could I without weeping see
This idolatrous display.

LYSANDER. Ah, my good, my gentle maid!
Thou art not my daughter, no,
'Twere too happy, if 'twere so.
But, O God! what's this I've said? —
My life's secret is betrayed!
'Twas my soul that spoke aloud.

JUSTINA. What do you say, sir?

LYSANDER. Oh! a crowd
Of old thoughts my heart hath stirred.

JUSTINA. Many times methought I heard
What but now you have avowed,
And yet never wished to hear,
At the risk perchance of paining,
A more accurate explaining
Of your sorrow and my fear;
But since now it doth appear
Right that I should be possess'd
Of the whole truth half confess'd,
Let me say, though bold appearing, —
Trust your secret to my hearing,
Since it hath escaped your breast.

LYSANDER. Ah! Justina, I have long
Kept this secret from your ears,
Fearing from your tender years
That the telling might be wrong;
But now seeing you are strong,
Firm in thought, in action brave,
Seeing too, that with this stave,
I go creeping o'er the ground,
Rapping with a hollow sound
At the portals of the grave,
Knowing that my time is brief,
I would not here leave you, no,
In your ignorance; I owe
My own peace, too, this relief:
Then attentive to my grief
Let your pleasure list.

JUSTINA. A fear

Struggles in my breast.

LYSANDER. Severe
Is the test my duty pays.

JUSTINA. From this most perplexing maze
Oh, sir, rescue me.

LYSANDER. Then hear.
I, most beautiful Justina,
Am Lysander . . . . This commencement
With my name need not surprise you;
For though known to you already,
It is right, for all that follows,
That it should be well remembered,
Since of me you know no more
Than what this my name presenteth.
Yes, I am Lysander, son
Of that city which on Seven
Hills a hydra seems of stone,
Since it seven proud heads erecteth;
Of that city now the seat
Of the mighty Roman empire,
Cradle of Christ's wider realm, —
Boon that Rome alone could merit.
There of poor and humble parents
I was born, if "poor" expresses
Well their rank who left behind them
Virtues, not vain earthly treasures.
Both of them by birth were Christians,
Joyful both to be descended
From brave sires who with their blood
Happily life's page had reddened,
Terminating the dull scroll
With death's bright emblazoned letters.
In the Christian faith well grounded

I grew up, and so well learnt it,
That I would, in its defence,
Even a thousand lives surrender.
I was young still, when to Rome,
In disguise and ill attended,
Came our good Pope Alexander,
Who then prudently directed
The high apostolic see,
Though its place there was not settled;
For, as the despotic power
Of the stern and cruel gentiles
Satisfies its thirst with blood
From the martyrs' veins that shed it,
So must still the primitive church
Keep concealed its sons and servants;
Not that they decline to die,
Not that martyrdom is dreaded
But that rebel rage should not,
At one stroke, one hour of vengeance,
Triumph o'er the ruined church,
So that no one should be left it
Who could preach and teach the word,
Who could catechise the gentile.
Alexander being in Rome,
I was secretly presented
To him there, and from his hand
Which was graciously extended,
With his blessing I received
Holy Orders, which the seraphs
Well might envy me, since man
Only such an honour merits.
Alexander, as my mission,
Unto Antioch then sent me,
Where the law of Christ in secret
I should preach. With glad contentment
I obeyed, and at their mercy,

Through so many nations wending,
Came at length to Antioch;
And when I, these hills ascending,
Saw beneath me in the valley
All its golden towers and temples,
The sun failed me, and down sinking
Drew with him the day, presenting
For my solace a companion,
And a substitute for his presence
In the light of stars, a pledge
That he'd soon return to bless me.
With the sun I lost my way,
And then wandering dejected
Through the windings of the forest,
Found me in the dim recesses
Of a natural bower, wherein
Even the numerous rays that trembled
Downward from each living torch
Could in noways find an entrance,
For to black clouds turned the leaves
That by day were green with freshness.
Here arranging to await
The new sun's reviving presence,
Giving fancy that full scope,
That wide range which it possesses,
I in solitude indulged
Many and many a deep reflection.
Thus absorbed was I in thought
When there came to me the echo
Of a sigh half heard, for half
To its owner retroverted.
Then collecting in mine ear
All my senses joined together,
I again heard more distinctly
That weak cry, that faint expression,
That mute idiom of the sad,

Since by it they're comprehended.
From a woman came that groan
To whose sigh so low and gentle
Followed a man's deeper voice,
Who thus speaking low addressed her:
"Thou first stain of noblest blood
By my hands this moment perish,
Ere thou meetest with thy death
'Neath the hands of infamous headsmen." —
Then the hapless woman said
In a voice that sobbed and trembled,
"Ah, lament for thine own blood,
But for me do not lament thee!" —
I attempted then to reach them,
That the stroke might be prevented,
But I could not, since the voices
At that moment ceased and ended,
And a horseman rode away
'Mong the tree-trunks undetected.
Loadstone of my deep compassion
Was that voice which still exerted
All its failing powers to speak
Amid groans and tears this sentence, —
"Dying innocent and a Christian
I a martyr's death may merit." —
Following the polar-star
Of the voice, I came directly
Where the gloom revealed a woman,
Though I could not well observe her,
Who in life's despairing struggle,
Hand to hand with death contended.
Scarcely was I heard, when she
Summoning up her strength addressed me, —
"Blood-stained murderer mine, come back,
Nor in this last hour desert me
Of my life." — "I am," said I,

"Only one whom chance hath sent here,
Guided it may be by heaven,
To assist you in this dreadful
Hour of trial." — "Vain," she said,
"Is the favour that your mercy
Offers to my life, for see,
Drop by drop the life-stream ebbeth,
Let this hapless one enjoy it,
Who it seems that heaven intendeth,
Being born upon my grave,
All my miseries should inherit." —
So she died, and then I . . .

## SCENE VIII.

LIVIA, JUSTINA, and LYSANDER.

Enter LIVIA.

LIVIA. Sir,
The same tradesman who so presses
To be paid, comes here to seek you,
By the magistrate attended.
That you were not in, I told him:
By that door you have an exit.

JUSTINA. This untimely interruption
By their coming, how it frets me!
For upon your tragic story
Life, soul, reason, all depended! —
But retire, sir, lest the justice
Should here meet you, if he enters.

LYSANDER. Ah! with what indignities
Poverty must be contented!
(Exit.

JUSTINA. They are coming here, no doubt,
Outside I can hear some persons.

LIVIA. No, they are not they. I see
It is Cyprian.

JUSTINA. How? what sendeth
Cyprian here?

## SCENE IX.

Enter CYPRIAN, CLARIN, and MOSCON.

CYPRIAN. A wish to serve you
Is the sole cause of my presence.
For on seeing the officials
Issuing from your house, the friendship
Which I owe unto Lysander
Made me bold herein to enter;
But to know ((Aside.) Disturbed, bewildered
Am I.) if by chance ((Aside.) What gelid
Frost is freezing up my veins!)
I in any way could help you.
((Aside.) Ah, how badly have I spoken! —
Fire not frost my blood possesses!)

JUSTINA. May heaven guard you many years,
Since in his more grave concernments,
Thus you honour my dear father
With your favours.

CYPRIAN. I shall ever
Be most gratified to serve you.
((Aside.) What disturbs me, what unnerves me?)

JUSTINA. He is not just now at home.

CYPRIAN. Thus then, lady, I can better
Tell you what is the true cause
That doth bring me here at present;
For the cause that you have heard
Is not that which wholly led me
Here to see you.

JUSTINA. Then, what is it?

CYPRIAN. This, which craves your brief attention. —
Fair Justina, beauty's shrine,
To whose human loveliness
Nature, with a fond excess,
Adds such marks of the divine,
'Tis your rest that doth incline
Hither my desire to-day:
But see what the tyrant sway
Of despotic fate can do, —
While I bring your rest to you,
You from me take mine away.
Lelius, of his passion proud,
(Never less was love to blame!)
Florus, burning with love's flame,
(Ne'er could flame be more allowed!)
Each of them by vows they vowed
Sought to kill his friend for you:
I for you disturbed the two,
(Woe is me!) but see the end;
While from death I saved my friend,
You my own death give in lieu.
Lest the scandal-monger's hum
Should be buzzed about your name,
Here to speak with you I came,
(Would that I had never come!)

That your choice might strike it dumb,
Being the umpire in the cause,
Being the judge in love's sweet laws; —
But behold what I endure,
While I their sick hearts may cure,
Jealousy mine own heart gnaws.
Lady, I proposed to be
Their bold spokesman here, that you
Might decide betwixt the two
Which you would select (ah, me!)
That I might (oh, misery!)
Ask you of your father: vain
This pretence. No more I'll feign: —
For you see while I am speaking
About them, my heart is seeking
But a vent for its own pain.

JUSTINA. Half in wonder and dismay
At the vile address you make me,
Reason, speech, alike forsake me,
And I know not what to say.
Never in the slightest way
Have your clients had from me
Encouragement for this embassy —
Florus never — Lelius no: —
Of the scorn that I can show
Let then this a warning be.

CYPRIAN. If I, knowing that you loved
Some one else, would dare to seek
Your regard, my love were weak,
And could justly be reproved.
But here seeing you stand unmoved,
Like a rock mid raging seas,
No extraneous miseries
Make me say I love you now.

'Tis not for my friends I bow,
So your warning hear with ease. —
To Lelius what shall I say?

JUSTINA. That he
Well may trust the boding fears
Of his love of many years.

CYPRIAN. To Florus?

JUSTINA. Not my face to see.

CYPRIAN. And to myself?

JUSTINA. Your love should be
Not so bold.

CYPRIAN. Though a god should woo?

JUSTINA. Will a god do more for you
Than for those I have denied?

CYPRIAN. Yes.

JUSTINA. Well then, I have replied
To Lelius, Florus, and to you.
(Exeunt JUSTINA and CYPRIAN at opposite sides.

## SCENE X.

CLARIN, MOSCON, and LIVIA.

CLARIN. Livia, heigh!

MOSCON. And Livia, ho! —
List good lass.

CLARIN. We're here, we two.

LIVIA. Well, what WANT you, sir? and YOU,
What do you want?

CLARIN. We both would show,
If perchance you do not know,
That we love you to distraction.
On a murderous transaction
We came here, to kill each other: —
So to put an end to the bother,
Just choose one for satisfaction.

LIVIA. Why the thing that you're demanding
Is so great, it hath bereft me
Of my wits. My grief hath left me
Without sense or understanding.
Choose but one! My heart expanding,
Beats so hard a strait to shun!
I one only! 'Tis for fun
That you ask me so to do.
For with heart enough for two,
Why require that I choose one?

CLARIN. Two at once would you have to woo?
Would not two embarrass you, pray?

LIVIA. No, we women have a way
To dispose of them two by two.

MOSCON. What's the way? do tell us, do; —
What is it? speak.

LIVIA. You put one out! —
I would love them, do not doubt . . . .

MOSCON. How?

LIVIA. ALTERNATIVELY.

CLARIN. Eh,
What's ALTERNATIVELY?

LIVIA. 'Tis to say,
That I would love them day about.
(Exit.

MOSCON. Well, I choose to-day: good-bye.

CLARIN. I, to-morrow, the better part.
So I give it with all my heart.

MOSCON. Livia, in fine, for whom I die,
To-day love me, and to-day love I.
Happy is he who so much can say.

CLARIN. Hearken, my friend: you know my way.

MOSCON. Why this speech? Does a threat lie in it?

CLARIN. Mind, she is not yours a minute
After the clock strikes twelve to-day.
(Exeunt.

## SCENE XI.

THE STREET BEFORE LYSANDER'S HOUSE: NIGHT

Enter FLORUS and LELIUS at opposite sides, not seeing each other.

LELIUS (aside). Scarcely has the darksome night
O'er the brow of heaven extended
Its black veil, when I come hither
To adore this sacred threshold;
For although at Cyprian's prayer,
I my sharp sword have suspended,
I have not my love, for love
Cannot be suspended ever.

FLORUS (aside). Here the dawn will find me waiting: —
Here, because 'tis force compels me
To go hence, for I, elsewhere,
Am away from my true centre.
Would to love the day had come,
And with it the dear, expected
Answer Cyprian may bring me,
Risking all upon that venture.

LELIUS (aside). I have surely in that window
Heard a noise.

FLORUS (aside). Some sound descends here
From that balcony.

## SCENE XII.

*The Demon appears at a window in the house of* LYSANDER.

LELIUS (aside). A figure
Issues from it, whose dim presence
I distinguish.

FLORUS (aside). Through the darkness
I can there perceive some person.

DEMON (aside). For the many persecutions

O'er Justina's head impending,
Her pure honour to defame
Thus I make a bold commencement.
(He descends by a ladder.

LELIUS (aside). But, O woe! what's this I witness! —

FLORUS (aside). What do I see! Oh, wretched! wretched! —

LELIUS (aside). From the balcony to the ground
The dark figure has descended.

FLORUS (aside). From her house a man comes forth! —
Jealousy kill me not, preserve me,
'Till I discover who he is.

LELIUS (aside). I will try to intercept him
And find out at once who thus
Tastes the bliss I've lost for ever.
(They advance with drawn swords to recognise the person who has descended.

DEMON (aside). Not alone Justina's fame
Do I by this act discredit,
But dissensions, perhaps murders,
Thus provoke. Ope, earth's dark centre,
And receive me, leaving here
This confusion
(He disappears between FLORUS and LELIUS, who meet together.

## SCENE XIII.

FLORUS and LELIUS.

LELIUS. Sir, whoever

You may be, it doth import me
To know who you are directly;
So at every risk I come here,
On this resolute quest determined.
Say who are you.

FLORUS. If the accident
Of my having been the observer
Of your secret love, compels you
To this valorous aggression,
More than it can you concern
Me to know, it doth concern me
To know you; for to be curious
Is far less than to be jealous.
Yes, by Heaven! for who is master
Of the house have I to learn here,
Who it is at such an hour,
By this balcony ascending,
Gaineth that which I lose weeping
At these gratings.

LELIUS. This excelleth,
Good, in faith, is it thus to dim
The clear light of my resentment,
By attributing to me
That which solely your offence is! —
Who you are I have to know,
Death to give to him who has left me
Dead with jealousy here, by coming
From this balcony.

FLORUS. How excessive
How superfluous is this caution,
Proving what it would dissemble!

LELIUS. Vainly would the tongue untangle

That which the keen sword can better
Thus cut through.

FLORUS. With it I answer.
(They fight.

LELIUS. In this way I'll know for certain
Who is the admitted lover
Of Justina.

FLORUS. My intention
Is the same. I'll die or know you.

### SCENE XIV.

Enter CYPRIAN, MOSCON, and CLARIN.

CYPRIAN. Gentlemen, I pray you let me
Interpose in this your quarrel,
Since by accident I am present.

FLORUS. You cannot oblige me more
Than by letting the fight be ended.

CYPRIAN. Florus?

FLORUS. Yes, for sword in hand,
I my name deny not ever
To who asks.

CYPRIAN. I'm at your side,
Death to him who would offend you.

LELIUS. You produce in me less fear,
Both of you thus joined together,
Than did he alone.

CYPRIAN. What! Lelius?

LELIUS. Yes.

CYPRIAN. I am prevented
(To Florus.
Now from standing at your side,
Since between you I present me.
How is this? In one day twice
Have I your disputes to settle! —

LELIUS. Then this time will be the last,
For we've settled them already;
Since in knowing who is he
Who Justina's heart possesses,
Now no more my hope remaineth,
Even the thought of it hath left me.
If you have not to Justina
Spoken yet, do not address her;
This I ask you in the name
Of my wrongs and my resentments,
Having seen her secret favours
Florus' happier fate deserveth.
From this balcony I saw him,
From my lost delight descending;
And my heart is not so base
As to meanly love, in presence
Of such jealousies so well proved,
Of disillusions, ah! so certain.
(Exit.

FLORUS. Stay.

## SCENE XV.

CYPRIAN. You must not follow him,
(Aside. (Oh, this news with death o'erwhelms me!)
Since if he who is the loser
Of what you have gained, expressly
Says he would forget it, you
Should not try his patient temper.

FLORUS. Both by you and him at once
Has mine own been too well tested.
Speak not now unto Justina
About me; for though full vengeance
I propose to take for being
Thus supplanted and rejected,
Every hope of her being mine
Now has ceased, for shameful were it,
In the face of such proved facts,
To persist in my addresses.
(Exit.

## SCENE XVI.

CYPRIAN, MOSCON, and CLARIN.

CYPRIAN (aside). What is this, O heavens! I hear?
Can it be the two are jealous
Of each other at one time?
And I too of both together? —
Doubtless from some strange delusion
The two suffer, which I welcome
With a sort of satisfaction,
For to it I am indebted
For the fact of their desisting
From their suit and their pretension. —
Moscon, have for me by morning

A rich court-suit; sword and feathers,
Clarin, be thy care; for love
In a certain airy splendour
Takes delight; for now no longer
Books or studies give me pleasure; —
Love they say doth murder mind,
Learning dies when he is present.
(Exeunt.

## ACT THE SECOND.

### SCENE I.

THE STREET IN FRONT OF LYSANDER'S HOUSE.

Enter CYPRIAN, MOSCON, and CLARIN, in gala dresses.

CYPRIAN (aside). Where, presumptuous thoughts, ah! where,
Would you lead me, whither go?
If for certain now you know
That the high attempts you dare
Are delusive dreams of bliss,
Since you strive to scale heaven's wall,
But from that proud height to fall
Headlong down a dark abyss?
I Justina saw . . . . . So near
Would to God I had not seen her,
Nor in her divine demeanour
All the light of heaven's fourth sphere.
Lovers twain for her contend,
Both being jealous each should woo,
And I, jealous of the two,
Know not which doth most offend.
All I know is, that suspicion,
Her disdain, my own desires,
Fill my heart with furious fires —

Drive me, ah! to my perdition.
This I know, and know no more,
This I feel in all my strait;
Heavens! Justina is my fate!
Heavens! Justina I adore! —
Moscon.

MOSCON. Sir.

CYPRIAN. Inquire, I pray,
If Lysander's in.

MOSCON. I fly.

CLARIN. No, sir, no. On me rely, —
Moscon can't go there to-day.

CYPRIAN. Ever wrangling in this way,
How ye both my patience try!
Why can he not go? Say why?

CLARIN. Because to-day is not his day.
Mine it is, sir, to his sorrow.
So your message I will bear.
Moscon can't to-day go there;
He will have his turn to-morrow.

CYPRIAN. What new madness can this be
Which your usual feud doth show?
But now neither of you go,
Since in all her brilliancy
Comes Justina.

CLARIN. From the street
To her house she goes.

## SCENE II.

Enter JUSTINA and LIVIA, veiled. — CYPRIAN, MOSCON, and CLARIN.

JUSTINA. Ah, me!
Cyprian's here. (Aside to her.) See, Livia, see!

CYPRIAN (aside). I must strive and be discreet,
Feigning with a ready wit,
Till my jealousy I can prove.
I will only speak of love,
If my jealousy will permit.
Not in vain, senora sweet, —
Have I changed my student's dress,
The livery of thy loveliness,
As a servant at thy feet,
Thus I wear. If sighs could move thee
I would labour to deserve thee;
Give me leave at least to serve thee,
Since thou wilt not let me love thee.

JUSTINA. Slight effect, sir, as I see,
Have my words produced on you,
Since they have not brought . . . .

CYPRIAN. Too true!

JUSTINA. A forgetfulness of me.
In what way must I explain
Clearer than I have done before,
That persistence at my door
Is and ever must be vain?
If a day, a month, a year,
If for ages there you stay,
Naught but this that now I say

Ever can you hope to hear.
As it were my latest breath,
Let this sad assurance move thee, —
Fate forbids that I should love thee,
Cyprian, except in death.
(She moves towards the house.

CYPRIAN. At these words my hopes revive: —
Sad! no, no, to joy they move me,
For if thou in death canst love me,
Soon for me will death arrive.
Be it so; and since so nigh
Comes the hour your words to prove —
Ah! even now begin to love,
Since I now begin to die.

(JUSTINA enters.

## SCENE III.

CYPRIAN, MOSCON, CLARIN, and LIVIA.

CLARIN. Livia, while my master yonder,
Like a living skeleton,
Life and motion being gone,
On his luckless love doth ponder,
Give me an embrace.

LIVIA. Stay, stay.
Patience, man! until I see,
For I like my conscience free,
If to-day is your right day. —
Tuesday, yes, and Wednesday, no.

CLARIN. What are you counting there? Awake!
Moscon's mum.

LIVIA. He might mistake,
And I wish not to act so.
For, desiring to pursue
A just course betwixt you both,
Turn about, I would be loth
Not to give you each his due.
But I see that you are right,
'Tis your day.

CLARIN. Embrace me, then.

LIVIA. Yes, again, and yet again.

MOSCON. Hark to me, my lady bright,
May I from your ardour borrow
A good omen in my case;
And as Clarin you embrace,
Moscon you'll embrace to-morrow!

LIVIA. Your suspicion is, in fact,
Quite absurd; on me rely.
Jupiter forbid that I
Should commit so bad an act
As to be cool in any way
To a friend. I will to thee
Give an embrace in equity,
When it is your worship's day.
(Exit.

## SCENE IV.

CYPRIAN, MOSCON, and CLARIN.

CLARIN. Well, I'll not be by to see,
That's a comfort.

MOSCON. How? why so?
Need I be chagrined to know,
If the girl's not mine, that she
Thus to you her debt did pay.

CLARIN. No.

MOSCON. This makes my point more strong,
Since to me it were no wrong
If it chanced not on my day.
But our master yonder, see,
How absorbed he seems.

CLARIN. More near,
If he speaks I'd like to hear.

MOSCON. And I, too, would like.

CYPRIAN. Ah me!
(As MOSCON and CLARIN approach CYPRIAN from opposite sides, he
gesticulates with his arms, and accidentally strikes both.
Love, how great thy agonies! —

CLARIN. Ah! ah, me!

MOSCON. Ah, me! I bawl.

CLARIN. Well, I think that we may call
This the land of the 'sigh-ah-mes'!

CYPRIAN. What! and have you both been here?

CLARIN. I, at least, was here, I'll swear.

MOSCON. And I, also.

CYPRIAN. O, despair
End at once my sad career!
Ah, what human heart to woe
Like to mine has given a home?

## SCENE V.

THE COUNTRY.

CYPRIAN, CLARIN, and MOSCON.

CLARIN. Whither Moscon, do we roam?

MOSCON. When we've reached the end, we'll know.
Leagues behind us lies the town,
Still we go.

CLARIN. A strange proceeding! —
Little time have we for reading,
Idly pacing up and down.

CYPRIAN. Clarin, get thee home.

MOSCON. And I?

CLARIN. Sly-boots, would you rather stay?

CYPRIAN. Go: here leave me both; away!

CLARIN. Mind, he tells us both to fly.

(Exeunt CLARIN and MOSCON.

## SCENE VI.

CYPRIAN. Memory of a maddened brain,
Do not with such strong control
Make me think another soul
Is what in my heart doth reign.
Blind idolator I have been —
Lost in love's ambitious flight,
Since such beauty met my sight,
Since a goddess I have seen.
Yet in such a maze of woe
Rigorous fate doth make me move,
That I know but whom I love,
And of whom I am jealous — no.
Yet this passion is so strong —
Ah, so sweet this fascination,
Driving my imagination
With resistless force along —
That I would (I know too well
How this madness doth degrade me)
To some devilish power to aid me,
Were it even to rise from hell,
Where some mightier power hath kept it, —
Sharing all its pains in common, —
I would, to possess this woman,
Give my soul.

## SCENE VII.

The Demon and CYPRIAN.

Demon (within). And I accept it.

(A great tempest is heard, with thunder and lightning.

CYPRIAN. What's this, ye heavens so pure?

Clear but a moment hence and now obscure,
Ye fright the gentle day!
The thunder-balls, the lightning's forked ray,
Leap from its riven breast —
Terrific shapes it cannot keep at rest;
All the whole heaven a crown of clouds doth wear,
And with the curling mist, like streaming hair,
This mountain's brow is bound.
Outspread below, the whole horizon round
Is one volcanic pyre.
The sun is dead, the air is smoke, heaven fire.
Philosophy, how far from thee I stray,
When I cannot explain the marvels of this day!
And now the sea, upborne on clouds the while,
Seems like some ruined pile,
That crumbling down the wind as 'twere a wall,
In dust not foam doth fall.
And struggling through the gloom,
Facing the storm, a mighty ship seeks room
On the open sea, whose rage it seems to court,
Flying the dangerous pity of the port.
The noise, the terror, and that fearful cry,
Give fatal augury
Of the impending stroke. Death hesitates,
For each already dies who death awaits.
With portents the whole atmosphere is rife,
Nor is it all the effect of elemental strife.
The ship is rigged with tempest as it flies.
It rushes on the lee,
The war is now no longer of the sea;
Upon a hidden rock
It strikes: it breaks as with a thunder shock.
Blood flakes the foam where helpless it is tost.

(The sound of the tempest increases, and voices are heard within.

VOICES WITHIN. We sink! we sink! we're lost!

DEMON (within). For what I have in hand,
I'll trust this plank to bear me to the land.

CYPRIAN. As scorning the wild wave
One man alone his life attempts to save.
While lurching over, mid the billows' swell,
The great ship sinks to where the Tritons dwell;
There, with its mighty ribs asunder rent,
It lies a corse of the sea, its grave and monument.

(Enter The Demon, dripping with wet, as if escaped from the sea.

DEMON (aside). For the end I wish to gain
It was of necessity
That upon this sapphire sea
I this fearful storm should feign,
And in form unlike that one
Which in this wild wood I wore,
When I found my deepest lore
By his keener wit outdone,
Come again to assail him here,
Trusting better now to prove
Both his intellect and his love. —
(Aloud.
Earth, loved earth, O mother dear,
From this monster, this wild sea,
Give me shelter in thy arms.

CYPRIAN. Lose, my friend, the dread alarms,
And the cruel memory
Of thy peril happily past;
Since we learn or late or soon,
That beneath the inconstant moon
Human bliss doth never last.

DEMON. Who are thou, at whose kind feet
Has my fortune cast me here?

CYPRIAN. One who with a pitying tear,
For a ruin so complete,
Would alleviate your woe.

DEMON. Ah, impossible! — for me
Never, never, can there be
Any solace.

CYPRIAN. How, why so?

DEMON. All my priceless wealth I've lost . . .
But I'm wrong to thus complain,
I'll forget, nay, think it gain,
Since my life it hath not cost.

CYPRIAN. Now that the wild whirl malign
Of this earthquake storm doth cease,
And the sky returns to peace,
Quiet, calm, and crystalline,
And the bright succeeds the dark
With such strange rapidity,
That the storm would seem to be
Only raised to sink thy bark,
Tell me who thou art, repay
Thus a sympathy so sincere.

DEMON. It has cost me to come here
More than you have seen to-day,
More than I can well express;
Of the miseries I recall
This ship's loss is least of all.
Would you see that clearly?

CYPRIAN. Yes.

DEMON. I am since you wish to know it,
An epitome, a wonder
Of all happiness and misfortune,
One I have lost, I weep the other.
By my gifts was I so glorious,
So conspicuous in my order,
Of a lineage so illustrious,
With a mind so well informed,
That my rare endowments feeling,
A great king (in truth the noblest
King of Kings, for all would tremble
If he looked in anger on them,)
In his palace roofed with diamonds
And with gems as bright as morning,
(If I called them stars, 'tis certain
The comparison were too modest,)
His especial favourite called me.
Which high epithet of honour
So enflamed my pride, as rival
For his royal seat I plotted,
Hoping soon my victor footsteps
Would his golden thrones have trodden.
It was an unheard-of daring,
THAT, chastized I must acknowledge,
I was mad; but then repentance
Were a still insaner folly.
Obstinate in my resistance,
With my spirit yet unconquered,
I preferred to fall with courage
Than surrender with dishonour.
If the attempt was rash, the rashness
Was not solely my misfortune,
For among his numerous vassals

Not a few my standard followed.
From his court, in fine, thus vanquished,
Though part victor in the contest,
I went forth, my eyes outflashing
Flames of anger and abhorrence,
And my lips proclaiming vengeance
For the public insult offered
To my pride, among his people
Scattering murder, rapine, horror.
Then a bloody pirate, I
The wide plains of the sea ran over,
Argus of its dangerous shallows,
Lynx-eyed where the reefs lay covered;
In that vessel which the wind
Bit by bit so soon demolished,
In that vessel which the sea
As a dustless ruin swallowed,
I to-day these fields of crystal
Eagerly ran o'er, my object
Being stone by stone to examine,
Tree by tree to search this forest: —
For a man in it is living,
Whom it is of great importance
I should see, this day expecting
The fulfilment of a promise
Which he gave and I accepted.
This infuriate tempest stopped me.
And although my powerful genius
Could chain up east, south, and north wind,
I cared not, as if despairing
Of success, with other objects,
Other aims in view, to turn them
To the west wind's summer softness. —
(Aside.
(I have said I could, but did not,
For I note the dangerous workings

Of his mind, and thus to magic
Bind him by these hints the stronger.)
Let not my wild fury fright thee,
Nor be at my power astonished,
For I could my own death give me,
If I were by rage so prompted,
And so great that power, the sunlight,
By my science could be blotted.
I, in magic am so mighty,
That I can describe the orbits
Of the stars, for I have travelled
Through the farthest and beyond them.
And in order that this boasting
May not seem to you mere bombast,
Look, if at this very instant
You desire it, this untrodden
Nimrod of rude rocks more savage
Than of Babylon is recorded,
Shall without a leaf being shaken,
Show the most horrific portents.
I am, then, the orphan guest here
Of these ash-trees, of these poplars,
And though what I am, assistance
At thy feet here I ask from thee:
And I wish the good I purchase
To repay thee with the product
Of unnumbered years of study,
Though it now slight effort costs me,
Giving to your wildest wishes
(Aside.
(Here I touch his love,) the fondest
Longings of your heart, whatever
Passion can desire or covet.
If through courtesy or caution
You should not accept my offer,
Let my good intentions pay you,

If from greater acts you stop me.
For the pity that you show me,
Which I thankfully acknowledge,
I will be a friend so faithful,
That henceforth the changeful monster
Of events and acts, called Fortune,
Which 'twixt flattering words and scornful,
Generous now, and now a miser,
Shows a friendly face or hostile,
Neither it nor that laborious
Ever flying, running worker,
Time, the loadstone of the ages,
Nor even heaven itself, heaven proper,
To whose stars the dark world oweth
All its most divine adornment,
Will have power to separate me
From your side a single moment,
Since you here have given me welcome.
And even this is almost nothing
When compared with what my wishes
Hope hereafter to accomplish.

CYPRIAN. Well to the sea, my thanks are due, that bore
You struggling to the shore,
And led you to this grove,
Where you will quickly prove
The friendly feelings that inflame my breast,
If happily I merit such a guest.
Then let us homeward wend,
For I esteem you now as an old friend.
My guest you are, and so you must not leave me
While my house suits you.

DEMON. Do you then receive me
Wholly as yours?

CYPRIAN (embracing him). This act doth prove it true,
That seals an eternal bond betwixt us two. —
(Aside.
Oh! if I could win o'er
This man to instruct me in his magic lore!
Since by that art my love might gain
Some solace for its pain;
Or yielding to its mighty laws
My love at length might win my love's sweet cause —
The cause of all my torment, madness, rage.

DEMON (aside). The working of his mind and love I gauge.

## SCENE VIII.

CLARIN and MOSCON enter running from opposite sides.
CYPRIAN and The Demon.

CLARIN. Oh! are you sir, alive?

MOSCON. My friend, do you
Speak civilly for once as something new?
That he's alive requires no demonstration.

CLARIN. I struck this lofty note of admiration,
Thou noble lackey, to express my wonder,
How from this storm of lightning, rain, and thunder,
Without a miracle he could survive.

MOSCON. Will you stop wondering, now you see him alive?

CYPRIAN. These are my servants, sir. —
What brings you here?

MOSCON. Your spleen once more to stir.

DEMON. They have a pleasant humour.

CYPRIAN. Foolish pair,
Their weary wit is oft too hard to bear.

MOSCON. This man, sir, waiting here,
Who is he?

CYPRIAN. He's my guest, so do not fear.

CLARIN. Wherefore have guests at such a time as this?

CYPRIAN (to The Demon). Your worth is lost on ignorance such as his.

MOSCON. My master's right. Are you, forsooth, his heir?

CLARIN. No; but our new friend there,
Looks like a guest, unless I deceive me, who
Will honour our poor house a year or two.

MOSCON. Why?

CLARIN. When a guest soon means to go away,
Well, he'll not make much smoke in the house, we say.
But this . . . .

MOSCON. Speak out.

CLARIN. Will make, I do not joke . .

MOSCON. What?

CLARIN. In the house a deuced deal of smoke.

CYPRIAN. In order to repair

The danger done by the rude sea and air,
Come thou with me.

DEMON. (Aside.) I'm thine, while thou hast breath.

CYPRIAN. I go to prepare thy rest.

DEMON (aside). And I thy death: —
An entrance having gained
Within his breast, and thus my end obtained;
My rage insatiate now without control
Seeks by another way to win Justina's soul.
(Exit.

CLARIN. Guess, if you can, what I am thinking about.

MOSCON. What is it?

CLARIN. That a new volcano has burst out
In the late storm, there's such a sulphur smell.

MOSCON. It came from the guest, as my good nose could tell.

CLARIN. He uses bad pastilles, then; but I can
Infer the cause.

MOSCON. What is it?

CLARIN. The poor gentleman
Has a slight rash on his skin, a ticklish glow,
And uses sulphur ointment.

MOSCON. Gad! 'tis so.
(Exeunt.

## SCENE IX.

THE STREET.

LELIUS and FABIUS.

FABIUS. You return, then, to this street.

LELIUS. Yes; the life that I deplore
I return to seek once more
Where 'twas lost. Ah! guide my feet,
Love, to find it! —

FABIUS. That house there
Is Justina's; come away.

LELIUS. Wherefore, when I will to-day
Once again my love declare.
And as she, I saw it plain,
Trusted some one else at night,
'Tis not strange, in open light,
That I try to soothe my pain.
Leave me, go; for it is best
That I enter here alone.
My rank in Antioch is known,
My father Governor; thus drest
In his robe as 'twere, my strong
Passion listening to no mentor,
I Justina's house will enter
To protest against my wrong.
(*Exeunt.*

## SCENE X.

A HALL IN THE HOUSE OF LYSANDER.

JUSTINA, and afterwards LELIUS.

JUSTINA. Livia . . . . But a step! who's there?

(LELIUS enters
LELIUS. It is I.

JUSTINA. What novelty,
What extreme temerity,
Thus, my lord, compels you? . . .

LELIUS. Spare
Your reproaches. Jealous-grown,
I can bear that you reprove.
Pardon me, for with my love
My respect has also flown.

JUSTINA. Why, at such a perilous cost
Have you dared . . .

LELIUS. Because I'm mad.

JUSTINA. To intrude . . . .

LELIUS. Heart-broken, sad.

JUSTINA. Here . . . .

LELIUS. Because, in truth, I'm lost.

JUSTINA. Nor perceive how scandal views
Such an act as now you do

'Gainst . . . .

LELIUS. Be not so moved, for you
Little honour now can lose.

JUSTINA. Lelius, spare at least my fame.

LELIUS. Ah, Justina, it were best
That this language you addressed
Unto him who nightly came
Down here from this balcony; —
'Tis enough for me to show
All your lightness that I know,
That less coy and cold to me
Your pretended honour prove.
If I am disdained, displaced,
'Tis another suits your taste,
Not that you your honour love.

JUSTINA. Silence, cease, your words withhold.
Who with insult e'er before
Dared to pass my threshold's door?
Are you then so blind and bold,
So audacious, so insane,
As my pure light to eclipse,
Through the libel of your lips,
By chimeras false and vain? —
In my house a man?

LELIUS. 'Tis so.

JUSTINA. From my balcony?

LELIUS. With shame
I repeat it.

JUSTINA. O, my fame,
O'er us twain your Aegis throw.

## SCENE XI.

THE SAME.

The Demon appears at the door which is behind JUSTINA.

DEMON (aside). For the deep design I handle,
For my double plot I come
Raging to this simple home,
Now to work the greatest scandal
Ever seen. Here, brooding o'er him,
This wild lover mad with ire,
I will fan his jealous fire,
I will place myself before him,
Catch his eye, and then as fleeing,
In invisible gloom array me.
(He affects to come in, and being seen by LELIUS muffles himself in
his cloak, and re-enters the inner apartment.

JUSTINA. Man, do you come here to slay me?

LELIUS. No, to die.

JUSTINA. What object seeing
Paralyses thus your senses?

LELIUS. What I see is your untruth.
Tell me now, the wish, forsooth,
Has invented my offences.
From that very chamber there
Came a man, I turned my head,
When he saw my face he fled

Back into the room.

JUSTINA. The air
Must this phantasy display —
This illusion.

LELIUS. Oh, that sight!

JUSTINA. Is it not enough by night,
Lelius, but in open day
Thus fictitious forms to see?

LELIUS. Phantom shape or real lover,
Now the truth I will discover.
(He goes into the room where The Demon had disappeared.

JUSTINA. I no hindrance offer thee,
For my innocence, a way,
At the cost of this permission,
Thus finds out the night's submission
To correct by the light of day.

### SCENE XII.

LYSANDER and JUSTINA; LELIUS, within.

LYSANDER. My Justina.

JUSTINA (aside). Woe is me!
Ah, if here before Lysander
Lelius from that room comes forth!

LYSANDER. My misfortunes, my disasters
Fly to be consoled by thee.

JUSTINA. What can be the grief, the sadness,

That your face betrays so plainly?

LYSANDER. And no wonder, when the pallor
Springs even from the heart. This sobbing
Stops my weak words in their passage.

(LELIUS appears at the door of the apartment.
LELIUS (aside). I begin now to believe,
Since he is not in this chamber,
Jealousy can cause these spectres.
He, the man I saw, has vanished,
How I know not.

JUSTINA (aside to Lelius). Come not forth,
Lelius, here before my father.

LELIUS. Convalescent in my sickness
I will wait till he is absent.
(Retires.

JUSTINA. Why this weeping? why this sighing?
What, sir, moves thee, what unmans thee?

LYSANDER. I am moved by a misfortune,
I'm unmanned by a disaster,
Greater far than tender pity
Ever wept, — the dread example
Cruelty has sworn to make
In the innocent blood of martyrs.
To the Governor of this city
Decius Caesar a strict mandate
Has despatched . . . I can speak no more.

JUSTINA (aside). What position e'er was harder?
Moved with pity for the Christians
Hither comes to me Lysander

The sad news to tell, not knowing
Lelius to his words may hearken, —
Lelius, the Governor's son.

LYSANDER. So Justina . . .

JUSTINA. Sir, no farther,
Since you feel it so acutely,
Speak upon this painful matter.

LYSANDER. Let me, for I'll feel some solace
When to thee it is imparted.
In it he commands . . .

JUSTINA. Proceed not
Further now, when you should rather
Cheat your years with more repose.

LYSANDER. How? when I, to make you partner
In those lively fears whose bodings
Are sufficient to despatch me,
Would inform you of the edict,
The most cruel that the margin
Of the Tiber ever saw
Writ in blood to stain its waters,
Do you stop me? Ah, Justina,
You were wont in another manner
Once to listen to me.

JUSTINA. Sir,
Different were the circumstances.

LELIUS (at the door, aside). I can hear but indistinctly
Half-formed words and broken accents.

## SCENE XIII.

FLORUS enters. — JUSTINA and LYSANDER; LELIUS, peeping at the door
of the inner room.

FLORUS (aside). Licence has a jealous lover,
Who but enters to unmask here
A pretended purity,
To forego politer manners.
I come here with that intention . . .
But as she is with her father
I will wait a new occasion.

LYSANDER. Who is there? Some footstep passes.

FLORUS (aside). Ah! 'tis now impossible
Without speaking to get back here.
Some excuse I'll try to offer: —
I am . . .

LYSANDER. You here, sir?

FLORUS. Your pardon.
I ask leave, sir, to speak with you
On a most important matter.

JUSTINA (aside). Oh! take pity on me, fortune,
For these trials are too many.

LYSANDER. Well, sir, speak.

FLORUS (aside, at the door). Florus in Justina's house
Leaves and enters like a master! —
These are not unfounded jealousies,
These are real and substantial.

LYSANDER. You grow pale, you change your colour.

FLORUS. Do not wonder, be not startled,
For I came to give a warning,
To your life of utmost value,
Of an enemy that you have,
Who your swift destruction planneth.
What I've said is quite sufficient.

LYSANDER (aside). Florus, doubtless, must have gathered
Somehow that I am a Christian,
And thus comes in kindliest manner
Of my danger to apprise me. —
(Aloud.
Speak, hide nothing in this matter.

## SCENE XIV.

LIVIA enters. — JUSTINA, LYSANDER, and FLORUS; LELIUS at the door of the room.

LIVIA. Sir, the Governor, who is waiting
At the door of the house, commanded
Me to call you to his presence.

FLORUS. Best I wait for his departure: —
(Aside.
(Meantime my excuse I'll think of.)
So 'tis well that you despatch him.

LYSANDER. I appreciate your politeness.
Here I will return instanter.
(Exeunt LYSANDER and LIVIA.

## SCENE XV.

JUSTINA and FLORUS; LELIUS at the door.

FLORUS. Are you then that virtuous maiden,
Who, the very breeze that flatters
With its soft and sweet caresses,
You would call rude, bold, unmannered?
How then is it you surrendered
Even the very keys of the casket
Of your honour?

JUSTINA. Hold, hold, Florus,
Do not dare to throw a shadow
On that honour which the sun
After the most strict examen
Has proved bright and pure.

FLORUS. Too late
Comes this idle boast. It happens
That I know to whom you have given
Free access . . .

JUSTINA. You dare this scandal? —

FLORUS. By a balcony . . .

JUSTINA. Do not say it.

FLORUS. To your honour.

JUSTINA. Thus will you blast me?

FLORUS. Yes, for hypocritical virtue
Merits something even harsher.

LELIUS (at the door, aside). Florus was not then the hero
Of the balcony; some more happy
Lover than us twain she welcomes.

JUSTINA. Oh! defame not noble damsels,
Since you noble blood inherit.

FLORUS. Noble damsel, dar'st thou call thee,
When thy very arms received him,
And from thy balcony he departed?
Power subdued thee; from the fact
That the Governor is his father,
Vanity led thee on to show
That in Antioch he commanded . . .

LELIUS (aside). Here he speaks of me.

FLORUS. Not seeing
Any graver defect of manner,
Than what in his birth and breeding
Rank may cover with its mantle,
But not so . . . .

(LELIUS enters.
LELIUS. Be silent, Florus,
Nor attack me in my absence;
For of a rival to speak ill,
Is the act but of a dastard.
'Tis to stop this I come forward,
Angry after so many passes
Which my sword has had with thine,
That I have not yet dispatched thee.

JUSTINA. Who, not guilty, ever saw her
In such dangerous straits entangled?

FLORUS. What behind your back was spoken,
I before you will establish,
Truth is truth where'er 'tis uttered.
(They grasp their swords.

JUSTINA. Florus! Lelius! what would you have then.

LELIUS. I would have full satisfaction
Where I heard th'insulting language.

FLORUS. I'll maintain what I have said
Where I said it.

JUSTINA. From so many
Strokes of fortune, free me, Heaven! —

FLORUS. And I'll learn to chastise your rashness.

## SCENE XVI.

The Governor enters with LYSANDER and attendants. —
JUSTINA, LELIUS,
and FLORUS.

(All who enter). Hold! stand back!

JUSTINA. Unhappy me!

GOVERNOR. What is this? But empty scabbards,
Naked swords, are quite sufficient
To inform me what has happened.

JUSTINA. What misfortune!

LYSANDER. What affliction! —

LELIUS. Ah, my lord . . .

GOVERNOR. Enough, no farther.
Lelius, thou a son of mine,
A disturber? Thou a scandal
To all Antioch through my favour?

LELIUS. Think, my lord . . .

GOVERNOR. Arrest, disarm them,
Take them hence. Make no distinction
On account of blood or rank here.
Let them suffer both alike,
Since in guilt alike they acted.

LELIUS (aside). I came jealous, and go outraged.

FLORUS (aside). To my pains new pains are added.

GOVERNOR. In distinct and separate prisons,
And with watchful eyes to guard them,
Place the two. — And you, Lysander,
Is it possible you have tarnished
Such a noble reputation,
Suffering . . . .

LYSANDER. No; let not these dazzling
False appearances mislead you,
For Justina in what happened
Was quite blameless.

GOVERNOR. In her house here,
Would you have her live regardless
Of the fact that they were young,
And that she was fair; My anger
I restrain, lest people say,

I, an interested party,
Sentence passed as partial judge. —
But of you who caused this quarrel,
Now that maiden shame has left you,
Well I know that you will glad me
With the occasion I desire,
Of exposing, of unmasking,
In the light of actual vices,
The false virtuous part you've acted.
(Exeunt The Governor and his attendants; LELIUS and FLORUS follow as prisoners.

SCENE XVII.

JUSTINA and LYSANDER.

JUSTINA. I reply but with my tears.

LYSANDER. Tears as vain as they are tardy.
What an act was mine, Justina,
When to thee my lips imparted
Who thou art! Oh, would I never
Told thee, that upon the margin
Of a rivulet in this forest,
A dead mother's womb here cast thee!

JUSTINA. I . . . .

LYSANDER. Do not attempt excuses.

JUSTINA. Heaven will make them, then, hereafter

LYSANDER. When too late, perhaps.

JUSTINA. No limit
Can be late here while life lasteth.

LYSANDER. For the punishment of crimes.

JUSTINA. Injured truth to re-establish.

LYSANDER. I, from what I have seen, condemn thee.

JUSTINA. I thee, from what thou knowest not, rather.

LYSANDER. Leave me; I go forth to die
Where my grief will soon dispatch me.

JUSTINA. At thy feet I would lose my life;
But do not reject me, father.
(Exeunt.

## SCENE XVIII.

A HALL IN CYPRIAN'S HOUSE.
At the end is an open gallery, through which is seen the country.

CYPRIAN, the Demon, MOSCON, and CLARIN.

DEMON. Since the hour that I have been
In your house a guest, you ne'er
Show a gay and cheerful air.
Sadness in your face is seen.
It is wrong your cure to shun,
Seeking to mislead mine eyes,
Since I would unsphere the skies,
Shake the stars, and shroud the sun,
For the least desire you feel
That more pleasantly you might live.

CYPRIAN. Magic has no power to give
The impossible I conceal,

Though the misery I betray.

DEMON. Come, confess the longed-for bliss.

CYPRIAN. I love a woman.

DEMON. And is this
The impossible that you say?

CYPRIAN. If you knew her, you'd agree.

DEMON. Well, describe her, I'm resigned;
Though I can't but smile to find
What a coward you must be.

CYPRIAN. The fair cradle of the skies,
Where the infant sun reposes,
Ere he rises, decked with roses,
Robed in snow, to dry heaven's eyes.
The green prison-bud that tries
To restrain the conscious rose,
When the crimson captive knows
April treads its gardens near,
Turning dawn's half frozen tear
To a smile where sunshine glows.
The sweet streamlet gliding by,
Though it scarcely dares to breathe
Softest murmurs through its teeth,
From the frosts that on it lie.
The bright pink, in its small sky
Shining like a coral star.
The blithe bird that flies afar,
Drest in shifting shades and blooms —
Soaring cithern of plumes
Harping high o'er heaven's blue bar.
The white rock that cheats the sun

When it tries to melt it down,
What it melts is but the crown
Which from winter's snow it won.
The green bay that will not shun,
Though the heavens are all aglow,
For its feet a bath of snow, —
Green Narcissus of the brook,
Fearless leaning o'er to look,
Though the stream runs chill below
In a word, the crimson dawn,
Sun, mead, streamlet, rosebud, May
Bird that sings his amorous lay,
April's laugh that gems the lawn,
Pink that sips the dews up-drawn,
Rock that stands in storm and shine,
Bay-tree that delights to twine
Round its fadeless leaves the sun,
All are parts which met in one
Form this woman most divine.
For myself, in blind unrest,
(Guess my madness if you can)
I, to seem another man,
In these courtly robes am drest,
Studious calm I now detest,
Fame no longer fires my mind,
Passion reigns where thought refined,
I my firmness fling to tears,
Courage I resign to fears,
And my hopes I give the wind.
I have said, and so will do,
That to some infernal sprite
I would offer with delight
(And the pledge I now renew)
Even my soul for her I woo.
But my offer is in vain,
Hell rejects it with disdain,

For my soul, it may allege,
Is a disproportionate pledge
For the interest I would gain.

DEMON. Is this, then your boasted courage,
In the footsteps of dejected
Swains to follow, who grow timid
When their first assault's rejected?
Are examples then so distant
Of fair ladies who surrender
All their vanities to entreaties,
All their pride to fond addresses?
Would you make your breast the prison
Of your love, your arms her fetters?

CYPRIAN. Can you doubt it?

DEMON. Then command them
To retire, those two, your servants,
So that we remain here only.

CYPRIAN. Go: both leave me for the present.

MOSCON. I obey.
(Exit.

CLARIN. And I as well. —
(Aside, concealing himself.
Such a guest must be the devil.

CYPRIAN. They are gone.

DEMON (aside). That Clarin's hiding,
Is to me of small concernment.

CYPRIAN. What more wish you now?

DEMON. First fasten
Well this door.

CYPRIAN. Yes; none can enter.

DEMON. For the possession of this woman,
With your lips you have asserted
You would give your soul.

CYPRIAN. 'Tis so.

DEMON. Then the contract is accepted.

CYPRIAN. What do you say?

DEMON. That I accept it.

CYPRIAN. How?

DEMON. So much have I effected
By my science, that I will teach you
How by it to get possession
Of the woman that you worship;
For I (though so wise and learned)
Have no other means to win her.
Let us now in writing settle
What we have resolved between us.

CYPRIAN. Do you wish by new pretences
To prolong the pains I suffer?
In my hand is what I tender,
But in yours is not the offer
That you make me; no, for never
Conjurations or enchantments
Can free will control or fetter.

DEMON. Give me, on the terms you spoke of,
Your signed bond.

CLARIN. (peeping). The deuce! This fellow
Is no fool, I see. No greenhorn
In his business is this devil.
I give him my bond! No, truly,
Though my lodgings wanted a tenant
For the space of twenty ages,
I wouldn't do it.

CYPRIAN. Sir, much jesting
May with merry friends be pastime,
Not with those who are dejected.

DEMON. I, in proof of what I am able
To effect, will now present you
With an example, though it faintly
Shows the power my art possesses.
From this gallery what is seen?

CYPRIAN. Much of sky, and much of meadow,
Wood, a rivulet, and a mountain.

DEMON. Which to you doth seem most pleasant?

CYPRIAN. The proud mountain, for in it
Is my adored one represented.

DEMON. Proud competitor of time,
Rival of the years for ever,
Who as king of fields and plains
Crown'st thee with the cloud and tempest,
Move thyself, change earth and air;
Look, see who I am that tell thee. —

And, look thou, too, since a mountain
I can move, thou mayest a maiden.

(The mountain moves from one side to the other in the perspective of
the theatre.

CYPRIAN. Never saw I such a wonder!
Ne'er a sight of so much terror!

CLARIN (peeping). With the fright and with the fear,
I enjoy a twofold tremble.

CYPRIAN. Mighty mountain bird that fliest,
Trees for wings replacing feathers,
Boat, whose rocks supply the tackle,
As thou furrowest through the zephyr,
To thy centre back return thee,
And so end this fear, this terror.

(The mountain returns to its original position.

DEMON. If one proof is not sufficient,
I will give you then a second.
Do you wish to see the woman
You adore?

CYPRIAN. Yes.

DEMON. Then, thy entrails
Ope, thou monster, to whose being
The four elements are servants.
Show to us the perfect beauty
That thou hidest in thy centre.
(A rock opens and JUSTINA is seen sleeping.
Is this she whom you adore?

CYPRIAN. Whom I idolize beyond measure.

DEMON. But since I have power to give her,
I can take her too, remember.

CYPRIAN. Now impossible dream of mine,
Now thy arms will be the centre
Of my love, thy lips the sun,
Burning, brimming as with nectar.

DEMON. Stay; for till the word you gave me
Is affirmed, and well attested,
You can touch her not.

(CYPRIAN rushes towards the rock, which closes.
CYPRIAN. Oh, stay
Cloud that hides the most resplendent
Sun, that on my bliss e'er dawned! —
But 'tis air my void arm presses. —
I believe your art, acknowledge
Now I am your slave for ever.
What do you wish I do for thee?
What do you ask?

DEMON. To be protected
By your signature here written
In your blood, at the foot of a letter.

CLARIN (peeping). Oh! I'd give my soul that I
To stay here had not been tempted.

CYPRIAN. For my pen I use this dagger,
Paper let this white cloth serve for,
And the ink wherewith I write it,
Be the blood my arm presents me.

(He writes with the point of a dagger upon a piece of linen, having
drawn blood from one of his arms.

CYPRIAN (Aside). Oh! I freeze with fear, with horror!
I, great Cyprian, say expressly
I will give my immortal soul,
(Oh! what lethargy, what frenzy!)
Unto him whose art will teach me
(What confusion! what strange terror!)
How I may of fair Justina,
Haughty mistress mine, possess me.
I have signed it with my name.

DEMON (aside). Now to my deceits is rendered
Valid homage, when such reason,
When discourse like his must tremble
Even when my help is sought for. —
Have you written?

CYPRIAN. And signed the letter.

DEMON. Then the sun you adore is thine.

CYPRIAN. Thine too, for the years eternal,
Is the soul I offer thee.

DEMON. Soul for soul I pay my debtors,
Then for thine I give to thee
Thy Justina's

CYPRIAN. In what term then,
Think you you can teach to me
All your magic art?

DEMON. A twelvemonth;

But on this condition . . . .

CYPRIAN. Speak.

DEMON. That within a cavern buried,
Without any other study,
We may live there both together,
In our service having no one
For us two but this attendant,
(Drags out CLARIN.
Who being curious hid him here; —
By securing thus his person
That our secret is well kept,
We, I think, may be quite certain.

CLARIN (aside). Oh, that I had never waited!
How does it happen though, so many
Neighbours prone to pry, as I am,
Are not caught thus by the devil?

CYPRIAN. So far well. My love, my genius
Have this happy end effected:
First Justina will be mine,
Then by my new lights, new learning,
I will wake the world's surprise.

DEMON. I have gained what I intended.

CLARIN. I not so.

DEMON. You come with us. —
(Aside.
O'er my great foe I've got the better.

CYPRIAN. Ah, how happy my desires,
If I reach to such possession! —

DEMON (aside). Never will my envy rest
Till I gain both souls to serve me. —
Let us go, and in the deepest
Cavern this wild world presenteth
You to-day will learn in magic
Your first lesson.

CYPRIAN. Let us enter,
For my mind with such a master,
For my love with such incentive,
Will the sorcerer Cyprian's name
Live before the world for ever.

## ACT THE THIRD.

### SCENE I.

A WOOD; AT THE EXTREMITY A GROTTO.

CYPRIAN.

CYPRIAN. Ungrateful beauty mine,
At length the day, the happy day doth shine —
My hope's remotest range,
The limits of my love and of thy change,
Since I to-day will gain
At last my triumph over thy disdain.
This lofty mountain nigh,
Raised to the star-lit palace of the sky,
And this dark cavern's gloom,
Of two that live, so long the dismal tomb,
Are the rough school wherein
From magic art its mystic lore I win,
And such perfection reach
That I can now my mighty master teach.

Seeing, that on this day, since I came here
The sun completes its course from sphere to sphere,
I from my prison cell come forth to view
What in the light I now have power to do.
Ye skies of cloudless day
List to my magic spell-words and obey;
Swift zephyrs that rejoice
In heaven's warm light, stand still and hear my voice;
Stupendous mountain rock
Shake at my words as at an earthquake shock;
Ye trees in rough bark drest
Be frightened at the groanings of my breast;
Ye flowers so fair and frail
Faint at the echoing terror of my wail;
Ye sweet melodious birds
Hush all your songs before my awful words;
Ye cruel beasts of prey
See the first fruits of my long toil to-day;
For blinded, dazzled, dazed,
Confused, disturbed, astonished and amazed,
Ye skies and zephyrs, rocks, and trees, and flowers,
And birds, and beasts, behold my magic powers,
And thus to all make plain
Cyprian's infernal study is not vain.

## SCENE II.

The Demon and CYPRIAN.

DEMON. Cyprian!

CYPRIAN. Wise friend and master still!

DEMON. Why, how is this, that using your free-will
More than my precept meant,
Say for what end, what object, what intent,

Through ignorance or boldness can it be,
You thus come forth the sun's bright face to see?

CYPRIAN. Seeing that now my spell
Can fill with fear, with horror even hell,
Since I, with so much care
Have studied magic and its depths laid bare,
So that yourself can scarcely tell
Whether 'tis I or you that most excel,
Seeing that now there is no place or part
That I with study, diligence and art,
have not attained,
Since necromancy's secret I have gained,
That art whose lines of gloom
Can ope to me the dark funereal tomb,
And bring before mine eyes
Each corpse that in it lies,
Regaining them, as 'twere by a new birth
From the hard avarice of the grasping earth.
The pale ghosts, one and all,
Rise and respond my call; —
And seeing that at length the sun
My goal of life had won,
Since from its innate force
Swift-speeding on its course,
Climbing the heavens each day,
It turns as 'twere reluctantly away,
And with a natural fear
Completes to-day the lifetime of a year,
I wish to attain the scope
To last of all my dreams, of all my hope.
To-day the rare, the beautiful, the divine
Justina will be mine,
Here summoned by my charms,
Here lured by love she'll come unto my arms,
For you from me no longer can require

Postponement of my hope's, my heart's desire.

DEMON. Nor do I wish to do it, no,
Since thus so earnestly you wish it so.
Now trace upon the ground
Mute mystic symbols, and the deep profound
Of air, with powerful incantations move
Obedient to your hope and to your love.

CYPRIAN. For that I will retire;
You soon shall see the heaven and earth admire.
(Exit.

DEMON. I give you leave to go,
Because our science being the same, I know
That the abyss of hell
Obedient to your spell
Will yield through me, this way,
The fair Justina to your arms to-day:
For, though my mighty power
Cannot enslave free-will even for an hour,
It may present
The outward show of rapture and content,
Suggesting thoughts impure: —
If force I cannot use, at least I lure.

## SCENE III.

CLARIN and The Demon.

CLARIN. Ungrateful fair, who still my heart doth hold,
Not burning Libya sure, but Livia cold,
The time is come to show
Whether in love you have been true or no,
Whether, since I within this cave was placed,
Not chased by me you have yourself been chaste;

For I have studied here
At second hand some magic for a year,
Just to find out (alack! I can't but wince)
Whether with Moscon you have wronged me since: —
Ye watery skies (some people call them pure)
List to my conjurations I conjure,
Mountains . . . .

DEMON. How, Clarin?

CLARIN. Oh! my master wise!
By the concomitance of my hands and eyes,
I've learned some magic, and would know by it
If Livia, that ungrateful little chit,
Has played me false since I have been away,
Embracing that rogue Moscon on my day.

DEMON. Have done with these buffooneries: leave me, go.
And 'mid these intricate rocks whose paths you know,
Assist your master, who will let you see
(If you would witness such a prodigy)
The end of all his woe.
I wish to be alone.

CLARIN. And I not so.
I now perceive
Why to use magic I have not your leave,
The fault was mine, neglecting to attest
My bond, and sign it with the blood of my breast. —
(He takes out a soiled pocket-handkerchief.
Upon this linen handkerchief
(None cleaner he can have who cries for grief)
I'll sign it now, the method I propose
Is but to give myself a box on the nose,
For there is little harm
Whether the blood is drawn from nose or arm.

(He writes with his finger on the handkerchief, after having drawn some blood.
I, the great Clarin, say, if I can level
Pert Livia's cruel pride, whom I give to the devil . . . .

DEMON. Leave me, I say again,
Go seek your master and with him remain.

CLARIN. Yes, I will do so, don't get angry though.
The reason you reject my bond I know:
'Tis this, because you see,
Do what I will that you are sure of me.

## SCENE IV.

The Demon.

DEMON. Abyss of hell prepare!
Thyself the region of thine own despair. —
From out each dungeon's dark recess
Let loose the spirits of voluptuousness,
To rain and o'erthrow
Justina's virgin fabric pure as snow.
A thousand filthy phantoms with thee brought
So people her chaste thought
That all her maiden fancies may be filled
With their deceits; let sweetest notes be trilled
From every tuneful grove,
And all, birds, plants, and flowers, provoke to love.
Let nothing meet her eyes
But spoils of love's delicious victories,
Let nothing meet her ears
But languid sighs that listening passion hears:
That thus unguarded by the faith, and weak,
She here may Cyprian seek
Invoked by his strong spell,

And by my blinding spirit lured as well.
Begin, in silence I will here remain
Unseen, that you may now begin the strain.
(Exit.

## SCENE V.

JUSTINA; music within. (They sing within.)

A VOICE. What is the glory far above,
All else that life can give?

CHORUS OF VARIOUS VOICES. Love love.

A VOICE. No creature lives on which love's flame
Has not impressed its burning seal,
The man feels more who love doth feel
Than when Life's breath first warmed his frame.
Love owns one universal claim, —
To Love, it only needs To Be, —
Whether a bird, a flower, a tree:
Then the chief glory, far above
All else in life must be . . . .

CHORUS (within). Love, love.

JUSTINA (alarmed and restless). Fancy, flatter that thou art,
Though thou should'st be sad to-day,
When did I to thee impart,
In this strange and sudden way,
Licence to afflict my heart?
What thus makes my pulses move?
What strange fire is this I prove
Which each moment doth increase?
Ah! this pain that ends my peace,
This sweet unrest, ah, what?

CHORUS. Love, love.

JUSTINA (more composed). 'Tis that enamoured nightingale
Who thus gives me the reply: —
To his partner in the vale
Listening on a bough hard by
Warbling thus his tuneful wail.
Cease, sweet nightingale, nor show
By thy softly witching strain
Trilling forth thy bliss and woe,
How a man might feel love's pain,
When a bird can feel his so.
No: it was that wanton vine
That in fond pursuit has sought
The tall tree it doth entwine,
Till the green weight it hath brought
Makes the noble trunk decline.
Green entwining boughs that hold
What you love in your embrace,
Make my fancy not too bold: —
Ah, if boughs thus interlace,
How would clasping arms infold! —
And if not the vine, 'twill be
That bright sunflower which we see
Turning with its tearful eyes
To its sun-god in the skies,
Whatsoe'er his movements be.
Flower thy watch no longer keep,
Drooping leaflets fold in sleep,
For the fond thought reappears,
Ah, if leaves can shed such tears,
What are those that eyes can weep!
Cease then, lyrist of the grove,
Leafy vine, unclasp thy arms,
Fickle flower, no longer move,

And declare, these poisoned charms
That you use, what yields?

CHORUS (within). Love, love.

JUSTINA. Love! it cannot be. Its chain
Have I ever worn for man?
No, the fond deceit is vain.
All received a like disdain,
Lelius, Florus, Cyprian.
Lelius did I not despise?
Florus did I not detest?
Cyprian, the good and wise,
(She pauses at Cyprian's name and resumes for a time her unquiet manner.
Spurn with such a haughty breast,
That he vanished from my eyes,
As if frightened by their ire? —
Where he went I do not know.
But save this, the faintest fire
Love e'er lit, ne'er dared to glow
In the depths of my desire.
Yes, for since I said that he
Should submit without appeal
Never more my face to see,
Ah, I know and what I feel! —
(She grows calmer.
Pity it must surely be,
That a man so widely known
Should through love of me be lost,
When he pays at such a cost
For the preference he has shown.
(She becomes troubled again.
Were it pity though, 'tis true,
The same pity I should give
Lelius and to Florus too,

Who in separate dungeons live,
Ah! for daring me to woo.
(She grows calmer.
But my thoughts, ye mutinous crew,
If my pity is enough
It should not be clogged by you.
Still your promptings press me so,
That I feel in my despair,
Where he is, if I could know,
I to seek him now would go.

## SCENE VI.

The Demon and JUSTINA.

DEMON. Come, and I will tell thee where.

JUSTINA. Who art thou who has procured
Entrance to this lone retreat,
Though the entrance is secured?
Or, my senses being obscured,
Art thou but delusion's cheat?

DEMON. No, not so; but having known
How this passion pressed thee so,
I have sought thee here alone,
Having promised thee to show
Whither Cyprian has flown.

JUSTINA. Then thou'lt reach not thy intent;
For this passion, this strange pain,
Which my thought doth so torment,
Though my fancy it may gain,
It will never my consent.

DEMON. But in thought to enter in

Shows that half the deed is done;
Since accomplished is the sin: —
Stop not halfway, ere is won
What the wish desired to win.

JUSTINA. Even in this desponding hour,
Though to think may taint the flower,
Thy suggestion comes to nought, —
In my power is not my thought
But my act is in my power.
I can follow to the brink,
Free to pause or to pursue,
Move my foot, or backward shrink,
For it is one thing to do,
And another thing to think.

DEMON. If a stronger power than thine,
Drawn from a profounder source,
With thine own desires combine,
How resist the double force
Which with force thy steps incline?

JUSTINA. I will trust a safer spell: —
My free will suffices me.

DEMON. But my power will it excel.

JUSTINA. Then the will no more were free
If a force could it compel.

DEMON. Come where every bliss thou'lt meet.
(Attempts to draw her with him, but cannot move her.)

JUSTINA. Ah! the bliss were bought too dear.

DEMON. It is peace, serene and sweet.

JUSTINA. 'Tis a slavery most severe.

DEMON. Life, 'tis joy.

JUSTINA. 'Tis death, deceit.

DEMON. Thy defence, what can it be,
If my power thus forces thee?
(Drags her with more force.

JUSTINA. In my God it doth consist.

DEMON. By persisting to resist,
(Releases her.
Woman, thou has conquered me.
Thy defence to God is due,
And my counsel is disdained;
Yes, but raging I'll renew
My attempt and have thee feigned,
If I cannot have thee true.
To a spirit I will give
Shape like thine though fugitive,
It will counterfeit thy form,
As with seeming life be warm,
And in it disgraced thou'lt live.
Thus two triumphs at one time
I am sure to win by this,
Be thy virtue so sublime,
Since through an ideal bliss
I will consummate a crime.
(Exit.

## SCENE VII.

JUSTINA.

JUSTINA. 'Gainst the clouds that round me lower
I appeal to heaven's high power;
Let this spectre of my fame —
As before the wind the flame —
As before the frost the flower,
Vanish, die . . . . But woe is me!
Who is here to heed my moan?
Was there not a man with me?
Yes. But no: I am alone:
No. But yes: for I could see.
Where so quickly could he fly?
Was he born of my unrest?
Oh! my danger's manifest . . .
Father! friend! Lysander! I
Call . . . .

## SCENE VIII.

LYSANDER and LIVIA enter from opposite doors. — JUSTINA.

LYSANDER. My child?

LIVIA. What means this cry?

JUSTINA. Saw you not a man (ah, me!)
Who but left me instantly?
I can scarce express my thought.

LYSANDER. A man here?

JUSTINA. You saw him not?

LIVIA. No, senora.

JUSTINA. I could see.

LYSANDER. Saw a man here? That is hard,
When the place was locked and barred.

LIVIA (aside). Moscon sure she must have seen,
Whom I have contrived to screen
In my changer.

LYSANDER. I regard
What you saw but as the play
Of your fancy and your fear.
Melancholy surely may
Have, the man that you saw here,
Formed from atoms of the day.

LIVIA. Yes, I think my master's right.

JUSTINA. No, 'twas no defect of sight,
No illusion: since my heart, —
Ah! too well I feel the smart —
Has been broken by the fright.
Some strange witchery of my will
Must have been effected here.
And with such consummate skill,
That if God had not been near
I might have pursued my ill.
He who at such timely hour
Helped me to resist the power
Of this fearful violence,
Will my humble innocence
Guard, whatever dangers lower. —
Livia, my cloak: whene'er

(Exit LIVIA.
Overwhelming griefs oppress,
I to holy church repair,
Where we secretly confess
The true faith.
(LIVIA returns with the cloak, which she places on JUSTINA.
LIVIA. 'Tis this you wear.

JUSTINA. There perchance I may appease
This strange fire that burns me so.

LYSANDER. I desire with thee to go.

LIVIA (aside). I will breathe much more at ease
When they're out of the house, I know.

JUSTINA. Since I wholly trust to thee
Heaven, thy hold to me afford.
Save me . . . .

LYSANDER. Come: so it may be.

JUSTINA. Since the cause is thine, O Lord!
Oh, defend Thyself and me!
(Exeunt JUSTINA and LYSANDER.

### SCENE IX.

MOSCON and LIVIA.

MOSCON. Have they gone?

LIVIA. They're gone: all right.

MOSCON. Why, I'm almost dead with fright.

LIVIA. Were you of your sense bereft
When but now my room you left
And appeared before her sight?

MOSCON. Left your room? Be seen by her?
Why, I swear it, Livia dear,
Not one moment did I stir.

LIVIA. Who then was it she saw here?

MOSCON. Well, the devil, as I infer.
How know I? But then do not
Take it so to heart, my soul.

LIVIA. Oh! that's not the cause.
(She weeps.

MOSCON. Then what?

LIVIA. Such a question, when the whole
Of a day it was his lot
With me here locked up to stay?
For his comrade far away
Must I not a tear then shed,
Though I take this day instead,
Having wept not yesterday?
Would I have him think of me
As a woman who could be
So forgetful and so frail,
As for half a year to fail
In what we did both agree?

MOSCON. Half a year? It is above
One whole year since he went away.

LIVIA. Quite an error, as I'll prove.

Mind, I cannot count a day
When I Clarin could not love.
This being so, if I to thee
Gave up half the year (ah me!),
I would give a false amount
To place all to his account.

MOSCON. Ah, ungrateful! can it be
When my heart on thee depends
For its peace, that thine attends
To such trifles?

LIVIA. Moscon, yes,
For I find, I must confess,
Short accounts make longest friends.

MOSCON. Such being then thy constancy,
Livia, I must say good-bye,
Till to-morrow. Ah! if he
Is thy two-day fever, I
Hope he's not thy syncope.

LIVIA. Well, my friend, from this you know
I no malice bear.

MOSCON. Just so.

LIVIA. See me then no more to-day,
But to-morrow, sir, you may:
I'll not need to send. Heigho!
(Exeunt.

## SCENE X.

A WOOD.

CYPRIAN, as frightened; CLARIN, stealthily after him.

CYPRIAN. Doubtless something must have happened
'Mong the stars; imperial clusters,
Since I find their influences
To my wishes so repugnant.
Up from the profound abysses
Some dark caveat must be uttered,
Which prohibits the obedience
Which they owe me as my subjects.
I, a thousand times, with spell-words
Made the winds of heaven to shudder,
I, a thousand times, the bosom
Of the earth with symbols furrowed,
Yet mine eyes have not been gladdened
By the human sun refulgent
That I seek, nor in mine arms
Hold that human heaven.

CLARIN. What wonder?
When a thousand times have I
Scraped the earth as if for nuggets,
When a thousand times the wind
By my screeching was perturbed,
And yet Livia was oblivious.

CYPRIAN. Once again then I am humbled
To invoke her thus. Oh, listen,
Beautiful Justina . . . .

## SCENE XI.

A phantom Figure of JUSTINA appears.

The Figure, CYPRIAN, and CLARIN.

FIGURE. Summoned,
As I wander through these mountains,
I obey a call so urgent.
What, then, wouldst thou? what, then, wouldst thou,
Cyprian, with me?

CYPRIAN. Oh, I shudder!

FIGURE. And since now . . . .

CYPRIAN. I am astonished!

FIGURE. I have come . . . .

CYPRIAN. What thus disturbs me?

FIGURE. To this place . . . .

CYPRIAN. What makes me tremble?

FIGURE. Where . . . .

CYPRIAN. Oh! whence this doubt that numbs me?

FIGURE. Love doth call me . . . .

CYPRIAN. Why, this terror?

FIGURE. And the powerful spell thou workest
Thus complied with, to this forest's

Deepest depths I fly to shun thee.
(Exit, covering her face with the cloak.

CYPRIAN. Listen, hear me, stay, Justina!
But why linger spell-bound, stunned here?
I'll pursue her, and this forest,
Whither by my spells conducted
She has flown, will be the leafy
Theatre, the rude-constructed
Bride-bed of the strangest bridal
Heaven e'er witnessed.
(Exit.

## SCENE XII.

CLARIN. Stop: Renuncio
Bride like this who smells of smoke
Stronger than a blacksmith's furnace.
But perhaps the incantation,
Being so extremely sudden,
Caught her leaning o'er the lye-tub,
If not cooking tripe for supper.
No. Thus cloaked and in a kitchen!
That excuse won't do: another
Let me try. (I have it now,
For an honourable woman
Never smells then any sweeter,)
She with fright must have been flustered. —
He has overtaken her now,
And from that rude vale uncultured,
Struggling in closed clasping arms,
(For I think when lovers struggle,
Open arms are not the weapon
Even for the lustiest lover,)
To this very spot they come:
I will watch them under cover,

For I wish for once to witness
How young women are abducted.
(Conceals himself.

## SCENE XIII.

CYPRIAN embracing the Figure of JUSTINA, which he carries in his arms.

CYPRIAN. Now, O beautiful Justina,
In this sweet and secret covert,
Where no beam of sun can enter,
Nor the breeze of heaven blow roughly,
Now the trophy of thy beauty
Makes my magic toils triumphant,
For here folding thee, no longer
Have I need to fear disturbance.
Fair Justina, thou hast cost me
Even my soul. But in my judgment,
Since the gain has been so glorious,
Not so dear has been the purchase.
Oh! unveil thyself, fair goddess,
Not in the clouds obscure and murky,
Not in vapours hide the sun,
Show its golden rays refulgent.
(He draws aside the cloak and discovers a skeleton.
But, O woe! what's this I see!
Is it a cold corse, mute, pulseless,
That within its arms expects me?
Who, in one brief moment's compass,
Could upon these faded features,
Pallid, motionless, and shrunken,
Have extinguished the bright beauties
Of the blush rose and the purple?

THE SKELETON. Cyprian, such are all the glories

Of the world that you so covet.
(The Skeleton disappears. CLARIN rushes in frightened, and embraces CYPRIAN.

### SCENE XIV.

CLARIN and CYPRIAN.

CLARIN. Fear, for any one who wants it,
Wholesale or retail I'll furnish.

CYPRIAN. Stay! funereal shadow, stay!
Now for other ends I urge thee.

CLARIN. I am a funereal body: —
Don't you see it by my bulk here?

CYPRIAN. Ah! who are you?

CLARIN. Who I am, sir,
Or am not, myself doth puzzle.

CYPRIAN. Did you in the air's void spaces,
Or earth's caverns yawning under,
See an icy corse here vanish,
See to dust and ashes turning
All the freshness and the beauty
That it promised in its coming?

CLARIN. Do you take me, sir, for one
Of those pitiful poor lurkers
Men call spies?

CYPRIAN. What could it be?

CLARIN. And not be, in such a hurry.

CYPRIAN. Let us seek it.

CLARIN. Let's not seek it.

CYPRIAN. I must sift this matter further.

CLARIN. I would rather not.

## SCENE XV.

The Demon, CYPRIAN, and CLARIN.

DEMON (aside). Just heavens,
If my nature, in conjunction,
Once possessed both grace and science,
When 'mongst angels I was numbered,
Grace alone is what I've lost,
Science no. Then why unjustly,
If 'tis so, deprive my science
Of its proper power and function?

CYPRIAN. Lucifer, wise master mine.

CLARIN. Pray don't call him: for he'll come here
In another corse, I warrant.

DEMON. Speak, what would you?

CYPRIAN. The annulling,
The redemption of those pledges,
At whose very thought I shudder.

CLARIN. As I don't redeem my pledges,
I'll slip off here through the bushes.
(Exit.

## SCENE XVI.

CYPRIAN and The Demon.

CYPRIAN. Scarcely o'er earth's wounded bosom
Had I the true spell-word uttered,
When in the ensuing action,
She, of all my dreams the subject,
My adored, divine Justina . . . .
But why take the useless trouble,
That to tell you know already?
I embraced her, would unmuffle
Her fair face, when (woe is me!)
In her beauty I discovered
A gaunt skeleton, a statue,
A pale image, a sepulchral
Show of death, which in these measured
Words thus spoke (even yet I shudder),
"Cyprian, such are all the glories
Of the world that you so covet." —
To assert, that on thy magic
As expressed by me, the burden
Of the fault should lie, is vain,
For I, point by point, so worked it,
That of all its silent symbols
There was not a line but somewhere
Had its place, of all its spell-words
Not one word that was not uttered.
Then, 'tis plain thou has deceived me,
For though acting as instructed,
I but found an empty phantom
Where I sought a blissful substance.

DEMON. Cyprian, this defect from thee,
Nor from me, in truth, resulted:

Not from thee, because the magic
Thou didst exercise with subtle
Thought and skill; and not from me,
For I could not teach thee further.
From a higher cause, believe me,
Came this injury thou hast suffered.
But be not cast down: for I,
Who in tranquil rest would lull thee,
Will to thee unite Justina,
By a different way and juster.

CYPRIAN. That is not my intention now.
For this strange event has struck me
With such terror and confusion,
That thy ways I do not covet.
And since thou has not complied with
The conditions, the assumptions
Of my love, I only ask thee,
Now that from thy face I'm rushing,
As the contract is annulled,
That my bond thou shouldst return me.

DEMON. What I promised was to teach thee,
By a course of secret study,
How to draw to thee Justina
By the potent power impulsive
Of thy words: and since the wind
Here Justina hath conducted,
I have then fulfilled my contract,
I have kept my plighted word then.

CYPRIAN. What was offered to my love
Was that I should surely pluck here
The sweet fruit whose seeds my hope
Had to these wild wastes entrusted.

DEMON. Cyprian, I was only bound
Her to bring here.

CYPRIAN. A mere shuffle:
To my arms you swore to give her.

DEMON. In thy arms I saw her struggle.

CYPRIAN. 'Twas a phantom.

DEMON. 'Twas a portent.

CYPRIAN. Worked by whom?

DEMON. By one who worked it
To protect her.

CYPRIAN. Who was he?

DEMON (trembling). I don't wish the name to utter.

CYPRIAN. I will turn my magic science
'Gainst thyself. By its compulsion
Speak, inform me who he is.

DEMON. Well, a god who takes this trouble
For Justina.

CYPRIAN. What's one God,
When of gods there's such a number?

DEMON. All their power in Him is centred.

CYPRIAN. Then One only, sole and sovereign,
Must He be, whose single will
Their united wills outworketh.

DEMON. I know nothing, I know nothing.

CYPRIAN. I renounce then with my utmost
Power the pact that I made with thee;
What compelled Him (this I urge thee
In that God's great name) to guard her?

DEMON (after having struggled ineffectually not to say it). To preserve her pure, unsullied.

CYPRIAN. Then He is the sovereign goodness
Since a wrong He will not suffer.
But if she remained here hidden
Say what loss would have resulted?

DEMON. Loss of honour, if the secret
Leaked out to the gossiping vulgar.

CYPRIAN. Then that God must be all sight,
Since he could foresee these trouble.
But, why could not thy enchantment
Be as potent and consummate?

DEMON. Ah! His power is ampler, fuller.

CYPRIAN. Then that God must be all hands,
Since whate'er He wills He worketh.
Tell me then who is that God,
Whom to-day I have discovered
The supreme of good to be,
The Creator, the Annuller,
The Omniscient, the All-seeing,
Whom I've sought for years unnumbered?

DEMON. Him I know not.

CYPRIAN. Speak, who is He?

DEMON. As I speak it, how I shudder!
He — He is the God of the Christians.

CYPRIAN. Say what moved Him to obstruct me
In my wish?

DEMON. Her Christian faith.

CYPRIAN. Does He guard so those who love Him?

DEMON. Yes; but now too late, too late,
Dost thou hope to gain His succour,
Since, in being my slave, thou canst not
Claim the privilege of His subject.

CYPRIAN. I thy slave?

DEMON. In my possession
Is thy signature.

CYPRIAN. I'll struggle
To regain it from thee, since
'Twas conditional at the utmost.
I don't doubt I will get it.

DEMON. How?

CYPRIAN. In this way.
(He draws his sword, strikes at The Demon, but cannot touch him.

DEMON. Although the lunges
Of thy naked sword against me

Are well aimed, thou hast not struck me,
Fierce as were thy blows. And now,
Even in more despair to plunge thee,
I would have thee learn at least
That the Devil is thy instructor.

CYPRIAN. What do you say?

DEMON. That I am he.

CYPRIAN. Oh! to hear thee how I shudder! —

DEMON. Not alone a slave art thou,
But MY slave; be that thy comfort.

CYPRIAN. I the slave of the Devil! I
Own a master so unworthy?

DEMON. Yes; for since thy soul thou gav'st me,
Thenceforth it to me was subject.

CYPRIAN. Is there then no gleam of hope,
No appeal, no aid, no succour,
By which I so great a crime
Can blot out?

DEMON. No.

CYPRIAN. Why doubt further?
Let not this sharp sword rest idly
In my hand, but swiftly cutting
Through my breast, become the willing
Instrument of mine own murder.
But what say I? He who could
Snatch Justina from thy clutches,
Can He not, too, rescue me?

DEMON. No. By choice thou wert a culprit,
And He does not favour crimes,
Virtues only.

CYPRIAN. If the summit
Of all power He be, to pardon
Is as easy as to punish.

DEMON. He rewardeth by His power,
He chastiseth from His justice.

CYPRIAN. One who yields He'll not chastise.
I am one, since I am humbled.

DEMON. Thou art mine, my slave: no master
Canst thou have but me.

CYPRIAN. I trust not.

DEMON. How, when still in my possession
Is that bond of thine, that bloody
Scroll inscribed by thine own hand?

CYPRIAN. He who is supreme and sovereign,
And depends not on another,
Will yet bear me through triumphant.

DEMON. In what way?

CYPRIAN. He is all sight,
And will see the fitting juncture.

DEMON. It I hold.

CYPRIAN. He is all hands,

And will burst my bonds asunder.

DEMON. Ere that comes I'll see thee dead:
Thus my clasping arms shall crush thee.

(They struggle together.

CYPRIAN. Thou great God, the Christians' God,
Oh, assist me in this struggle!

DEMON (flinging CYPRIAN from his arms). It is He who has saved thy life.

CYPRIAN. More He'll do since I seek Him humbly.
(Exeunt.

## SCENE XVII.

HALL IN THE PALACE OF THE GOVERNOR.

The Governor, FABIUS, and Soldiers.

GOVERNOR. How then was the capture made?

FABIUS. In their church, as we suspected,
We discovered them collected,
Where before their God they prayed.
With an armed guard I traced them
To this secret sacred hall,
Made them prisoners one and all,
And in different prisons placed them.
But, your patience not to tire,
The chief point I may declare, —
Captured is Justina fair,
And Lysander her old sire.

GOVERNOR. If for gold, a fair pretence,
If for rank, you would not miss,
Wherefore bring me news like this
And not claim your recompense?

FABIUS. If you deign to value thus
My poor service you may pay it.

GOVERNOR. How?

FABIUS. With great respect I say it,
Florus free, and Lelius.

GOVERNOR. Though I seemed austere and cold,
Them chastising without pity
To strike terror through the city,
Yet if the whole truth were told,
Then the cause were plain why they
Have been prisoned a whole year.
It is this, a father's fear
Lelius would preserve this way.
Florus was his rival, he
Had a host of powerful friends,
Each was jealous, and his ends
Would attain whate'er might be.
I was fearful a collision
Would ensue if they should meet,
So I thought it more discreet
Not to come to a decision.
So with this intent I sought
Some pretext, Justina's face
To expel from out this place,
But I could discover nought.
But since this event to-day,
With her damaged character,
Gives a right to banish her,

Nay, to take her life away,
Let them be released. No fear
Need you have about their fate;
Go, and Lelius liberate,
Go, and Florus bring me here.

FABIUS. Myriad times I kiss thy feet
For a favour so immense.
(Exit.

## SCENE XVIII.

The Governor and Soldiers.

GOVERNOR. And since now this fair pretence,
This hypocritical deceit,
In my power at last doth lie,
Wherefore my revenge postpone
For the sorrows I have known
Through her fault? Yes, she shall die
By the bloody headsman's hand.
(To a Soldier.
Bring her hither in my name.
Let her punishment and shame
Be a terror to the land.
Let the palace she thought sweet
But her scaffold scene present.
(Exit the Soldier with others.

## SCENE XIX.

FABIUS, LELIUS, and FLORUS. — THE SAME.

FABIUS. Sir, the two for whom you sent
Here are kneeling at your feet.

LELIUS. I, whose wish it is to be
Welcomed as thy son this time,
With no consciousness of crime
Do not see a judge in thee,
I an angry sire may see
With a son's respectful fear
And obedience.

FLORUS. Being here, I infer that it must be
(Though no guilt can I discern)
Thy chastising hand to feel.
See. Submissive here I kneel.

GOVERNOR. Lelius, Florus, I was stern,
Justly stern against ye two,
For as judge or father I
Could not unchastised pass by
Your offence. But then I knew
That in noble hearts the feeling
Of resentment does not last,
And as now the cause is past,
I resolved, to both appealing,
Friends to make of you once more.
So to consecrate the tie
Now embrace in amity.

LELIUS. I am glad that, as of yore,
Florus is my friend to-day.

FLORUS. That thou'rt mine this act may show.
Here's my hand.

GOVERNOR. This being so,
You are free to go or stay: —
When I tell you of the sad
Fall of her you once admired,

Northing further is required.

## SCENE XX.

The Demon, a crowd of People. — THE SAME.

DEMON (within). Ware! beware! He's mad! he's mad!

GOVERNOR. What is this?

LELIUS. I'll go and see.
(He goes to the door, and after a pause returns.

GOVERNOR. In this palace hall these cries,
From what cause can they arise?

FLORUS. Something serious it must be.

LELIUS. This confusion is occasioned
(Hear a singular adventure),
Sir, by Cyprian, who being absent
Many days again has entered
Antioch completely mad.

FLORUS. It was doubtless the fine essence
Of his mind that thus has brought him
To this lamentable ending.

PEOPLE (within). Ware the madman! ware the madman!

## SCENE XXI.

CYPRIAN, half naked; People. — THE SAME.

CYPRIAN. Never was I more collected;
It is you yourselves are mad.

GOVERNOR. Cyprian, what is all this ferment?

CYPRIAN. Governor of Antioch,
Viceroy of great Caesar Decius,
Florus, Lelius, my young friends,
Whom I valued and respected,
Proud nobility, great people,
To my words be all attentive:
I am Cyprian, I am he
Once so studious, and so learned,
I the wonder of the schools,
Of the sciences the centre.
What I gained from all my studies
Was one doubt, a doubt that never
Left my wildered mind a moment,
Ever troubling and perplexing.
I Justina saw, and seeing,
To her charms my soul surrendered,
And for soft voluptuous Venus
Left the wise and learn'd Minerva.
Baffled by Justina's virtue,
I, pursuing though rejected,
And from one extreme to another
Passing on as passion led me,
To my guest, who from the sea
Found my feet a port of shelter,
For Justina pledged my soul,
Since at once he charmed my senses
And my intellect, by giving
Love its hopes, and thought its treasures.
From that hour, as his disciple
Lived I in these lonely deserts,
And to his laborious teaching
I am for a power indebted,
By which I can move even mountains

And in different places set them:
Yet although these mighty wonders
I can do to-day, I'm helpless
By the voice of my desire
To draw towards me one fair vestal.
And the cause why I am powerless
To subdue that beauteous virgin
Is that by a God she's guarded,
Whom, now knowing by His blessed
Grace bestowed, I come to acknowledge
As the Infinite, the Eternal.
Yes, the great God of the Christians
I now openly confess here.
And though true it is I am
Still of hell the slave and servant,
Having with my very blood
Signed a certain secret cedule,
Yet my blood that blood may blot out
In the martyrdom I'm expecting.
If you are a judge, if Christians
You pursue with bloody vengeance,
I am one: for in these mountains
A grave venerable elder
The first sacrament conferring
With its sacred sign impressed me.
This being so, why wait? Your orders
Give unto the bloody headsman,
Tell him here to strike this neck
And from it my head dissever.
Try my firmness as you will,
For I, resolute and determined,
Will endure a thousand deaths
Since this truth at last I've learned,
That without the great God, whom
Now I seek, adore, and reverence,
Human glories are but ashes,

Dust, smoke, wind, delusive, empty.
(He falls as if in a swoon, with his face to the ground.

GOVERNOR. So absorbed, so lost in wonder,
Cyprian, has thy daring left me,
That considering modes of torture
I have yet not one selected.
Rise. Bestir thee.
(Spurns him with his foot.

FLORUS. As a statue
Formed of ice he lies extended

SCENE XXII.

Soldiers, JUSTINA. — THE SAME.

A SOLDIER. Here, your Highness, is Justina.

GOVERNOR (aside). I must go, her face unnerves me. —
With this living corse here lying
(Aside to his retinue.
Let us leave her for the present.
For the two being here confined,
It may alter their intentions,
Seeing that they are condemned
Both to die: if not, 'tis certain,
That unless they adore our gods
Frightful torments soon shall end them.

LELIUS (aside). I remain 'twixt love and fear
Quite bewildered and suspended.

FLORUS (aside). So affected have I been,
I scarce know what most affects me.

(Exeunt all, except JUSTINA.

## SCENE XXIII.

JUSTINA; CYPRIAN, insensible on the ground.

JUSTINA. What! without a word you leave me?
When I come here, calm, contented,
Even to die. Ah! wishing death,
Am I then of death prevented? —
(She perceives CYPRIAN.
But my punishment is, doubtless,
Thus locked up to face the terrors
Of a slow and lingering death,
With the body of this wretch here
Left alone, my sole companion
Being a corse. O thou, re-entered
Into thy original earth,
Happy wert thou, if thy sentence
Was passed on thee for the faith
I adore!

CYPRIAN (recovering consciousness). O proud avenger
Of your gods, why wait, the thread
Of my life to cut? . . .
(He perceives JUSTINA, and rises.
 Heaven bless me! —
(Aside.
Can I trust my eyes? Justina!

JUSTINA (aside). Cyprian, do I see? O Heaven!

CYPRIAN (aside). No, it is not she, my thought
Fills the void air with her presence.

JUSTINA (aside). No, it is not he, the wind

Forms this phantom to divert me.

CYPRIAN. Shadow of my fantasy . . .

JUSTINA. Of my wish, delusive spectre . . .

CYPRIAN. Terror of my startled senses . . .

JUSTINA. Horror of my heart's dejection . . .

CYPRIAN. What, then, wouldst thou?

JUSTINA. What, then, wouldst thou?

CYPRIAN. I invoked thee not. What errand
Has thou come on?

JUSTINA. Why thus seek me?
I to thee no thought directed.

CYPRIAN. Ah! I sought thee not, Justina.

JUSTINA. Nor here at thy call I entered.

CYPRIAN. Then why here?

JUSTINA. I am a prisoner. —
Thou?

CYPRIAN. I, too, have been arrested.
But, Justina, say what crime
Could thy virtue have effected?

JUSTINA. It is not for any crime,
It is from their deep resentment,
Their abhorrence of Christ's faith,

Whom I as my God confess here.

CYPRIAN. Thou dost owe Him that, Justina,
For thy God was thy defender,
He watched o'er thee in His goodness.
Get my prayers to Him accepted.

JUSTINA. Pray with faith, and He will listen.

CYPRIAN. Then with that I will address Him.
Though a fear, that's not despair,
Makes me for my great sins tremble.

JUSTINA. Oh! have confidence.

CYPRIAN. My crimes are
So immense.

JUSTINA. But more immense are
His great mercies.

CYPRIAN. Then, will He
Pardon have on me?

JUSTINA. 'Tis certain.

CYPRIAN. How, if my soul surrendered
To the Demon's self, as purchase
Of thy beauty?

JUSTINA. Oh, there are not
Stars as many in the heavens,
Sands as many on the shore,
Sparks within the fire as many,
Motes as many in the beam,
On the winds so many feathers,

As the sins He can forgive.

CYPRIAN. I believe it, and am ready
Now a thousand lives to give Him. —
But I hear some people enter.

### SCENE XXIV.

FABIUS, leading in MOSCON, CLARIN, and LIVIA, as prisoners; CYPRIAN and JUSTINA.

FABIUS. With your master and your mistress
Here remain confined together.
(Exit.

LIVIA. If THEY fancy to be Christians,
What have WE done to offend them?

MOSCON. Much: 'tis crime enough for us
That we happen to be servants.

CLARIN. Flying peril in the mountain,
I find here a greater peril.

### SCENE XXV.

A Servant. — THE SAME.

SERVANT. The Lord Governor Aurelius
Summons Cyprian to his presence,
And Justina.

JUSTINA. Ah! how happy,
If 'tis for the wished-for ending.
Do not, Cyprian, be disheartened.

CYPRIAN. Faith, zeal, courage, all possess me:
For if life must be the ransom
Of my slavery to the devil,
He who gave his soul for thee,
Will he not give God his person?

JUSTINA. I once said that I could love thee
But in death, and since together,
Cyprian, we now must die,
What I promised I present thee.

(They are led out by the Servant.

## SCENE XXVI.

MOSCON, LIVIA, and CLARIN.

MOSCON. How contentedly to die
They go forth.

LIVIA. Much more contented
Are we three to remain alive.

CLARIN. Not much more; for we must settle
Our account now, though I own
The occasion might be better,
And the place too, still 'twere wrong
To neglect the time that's present.

MOSCON. What account pray?

CLARIN. I have been
Absent.

LIVIA. Speak.

CLARIN. The whole of a twelvemonth,
When without my intermission
Moscon in possession held thee.
Now my quota in the business,
If we both have equal measure,
Is that I must have my year.

LIVIA. Can it be that I'm suspected
Of thus wronging thee so basely?
Why, I wept whole days together
When it was the day for weeping.

MOSCON. Yes, for I myself was present:
Every day that was not mine
She thy friendship quite respected.

CLARIN. That's a bounce; for not a tear,
When this day her house I entered,
Did she shed, and there I found thee
Sitting with her quite contented.

LIVIA. But this day is not a fast.

CLARIN. Yes, it is; for I remember
That the day I went away
Was my day.

LIVIA. Oh! that's an error.

MOSCON. Yes, I see how that arises,
This year is a year bissextile,
And our days are now the same.

CLARIN. Well, I'm satisfied, 'tis better
That a man should not too deeply

Pry into such things. — Good heavens! —

(The sound of a great tempest is heard.

## SCENE XXVII.

The Governor, a crowd of People; then FABIUS, LELIUS, and FLORUS, all
astonished; afterwards The Demon.

LIVIA. Sure the house is tumbling down.

MOSCON. How terrific! what a tempest!

GOVERNOR. Doubtless in disastrous ruin
Topple down the walls of heaven

(The tempest is renewed, and enter FABIUS, LELIUS, and FLORUS.

FABIUS. Scarcely on the public scaffold
Had the headsman's hand dissevered
Cyprian and Justina's necks,
When the earth, even to its centre,
Seemed to tremble.

LELIUS. And a cloud,
From whose burning womb extended
The wild lightnings, the loud thunders,
Awful embryos were projected,
Fell upon us.

FLORUS. From which issued
A most horrid, most repelling
Shape, who on the scaly shells
Of a mailed and mighty serpent,

O'er the scaffold made a sign
Motioning silence and attention.

(The Scene opens, and a scaffold with the heads and bodies of
JUSTINA and CYPRIAN is seen. Over it in the air, upon a
winged serpent, is
The Demon.

DEMON. Hear, O mortals, hear what I,
By the orders of high Heaven,
For Justina's exculpation,
Must declare to all here present.
I it was, who to dishonour
Her pure fame, in form dissembled
For the purpose, scaled her house,
And her very chamber entered.
And in order that her fame
Should not by that fraud be lessened,
I come here her injured honour
To exhibit pure and perfect.
Cyprian, who with her lieth
On a happy bier at rest there,
Was my slave. But he effacing,
With the blood his neck outsheddeth,
The red signature, the linen
Is now spotless and unblemished.
And the two, in spite of me,
Having to the spheres ascended
Of the sacred throne of God,
Live there in a world far better. —
This, then, is the truth, which I
Tell, because God makes me tell it,
Much against my will, my practice
Not being great as a truth-teller.
(He falls swiftly, and sinks into the earth.

LIVIA. Oh! what horror!

FLORUS. What confusion!

LIVIA. What a prodigy!

MOSCON. What terror!

GOVERNOR. These are all but the enchantments
Which this sorcerer effected
At his death.

FLORUS. I am in doubt
To believe them or reject them.

LELIUS. The mere thought of them confounds me.

CLARIN. If magician, it is certain,
As I hold, he must have been
The magician then of heaven.

MOSCON. Leaving our partitioned love
In a rather odd dilemma,
For "The Wonderful Magician"
Ask the pardon of its errors.

END

# LIFE IS A DREAM

## Translated by Edward Fitzgerald

PERSONS

Basilio King of Poland.
Segismund his Son.
Astolfo his Nephew.
Estrella his Niece.
Clotaldo a General in Basilio's Service.
Rosaura a Muscovite Lady.
Fife her Attendant.

Chamberlain, Lords in Waiting, Officers, Soldiers, etc., in Basilio's Service.

The Scene of the first and third Acts lies on the Polish frontier: o the second Act, in Warsaw.

## ACT THE FIRST

### SCENE I

A pass of rocks, over which a storm is rolling away, and the sun setting: in the foreground, half-way down, a fortress.

(Enter first from the topmost rock Rosaura, as from horseback, in man's attire; and, after her, Fife.)

ROSAURA. There, four-footed Fury, blast
Engender'd brute, without the wit
Of brute, or mouth to match the bit
Of man — art satisfied at last?
Who, when thunder roll'd aloof,
Tow'rd the spheres of fire your ears

    Pricking, and the granite kicking
    Into lightning with your hoof,
    Among the tempest-shatter'd crags
    Shattering your luckless rider
    Back into the tempest pass'd?
    There then lie to starve and die,
    Or find another Phaeton
    Mad-mettled as yourself; for I,
    Wearied, worried, and for-done,
    Alone will down the mountain try,
    That knits his brows against the sun.

FIFE (as to his mule). There, thou mis-begotten thing,
    Long-ear'd lightning, tail'd tornado,
    Griffin-hoof-in hurricano,
    (I might swear till I were almost
    Hoarse with roaring Asonante)
    Who forsooth because our betters
    Would begin to kick and fling
    You forthwith your noble mind
    Must prove, and kick me off behind,
    Tow'rd the very centre whither
    Gravity was most inclined.
    There where you have made your bed
    In it lie; for, wet or dry,
    Let what will for me betide you,
    Burning, blowing, freezing, hailing;
    Famine waste you: devil ride you:
    Tempest baste you black and blue:
    (To Rosaura.)
    There! I think in downright railing
    I can hold my own with you.

ROS. Ah, my good Fife, whose merry loyal pipe,
    Come weal, come woe, is never out of tune
    What, you in the same plight too?

FIFE. Ay; And madam — sir — hereby desire,
  When you your own adventures sing
  Another time in lofty rhyme,
  You don't forget the trusty squire
  Who went with you Don-quixoting.

ROS. Well, my good fellow — to leave Pegasus
  Who scarce can serve us than our horses worse —
  They say no one should rob another of
  The single satisfaction he has left
  Of singing his own sorrows; one so great,
  So says some great philosopher, that trouble
  Were worth encount'ring only for the sake
  Of weeping over — what perhaps you know
  Some poet calls the 'luxury of woe.'

FIFE. Had I the poet or philosopher
  In the place of her that kick'd me off to ride,
  I'd test his theory upon his hide.
  But no bones broken, madam — sir, I mean? —

ROS. A scratch here that a handkerchief will heal —
  And you? —

FIFE. A scratch in *quiddity*, or kind:
  But not in '*quo*' — my wounds are all behind.
  But, as you say, to stop this strain,
  Which, somehow, once one's in the vein,
  Comes clattering after — there again! —
  What are we twain — deuce take't! — we two,
  I mean, to do — drench'd through and through —
  Oh, I shall choke of rhymes, which I believe
  Are all that we shall have to live on here.

ROS. What, is our victual gone too? —

FIFE. Ay, that brute
 Has carried all we had away with her,
 Clothing, and cate, and all.

ROS. And now the sun,
 Our only friend and guide, about to sink
 Under the stage of earth.

FIFE. And enter Night,
 With Capa y Espada — and — pray heaven!
 With but her lanthorn also.

ROS. Ah, I doubt
 To-night, if any, with a dark one — or
 Almost burnt out after a month's consumption.
 Well! well or ill, on horseback or afoot,
 This is the gate that lets me into Poland;
 And, sorry welcome as she gives a guest
 Who writes his own arrival on her rocks
 In his own blood —
 Yet better on her stony threshold die,
 Than live on unrevenged in Muscovy.

FIFE. Oh, what a soul some women have — I mean
 Some men —

ROS. Oh, Fife, Fife, as you love me, Fife,
 Make yourself perfect in that little part,
 Or all will go to ruin!

FIFE. Oh, I will,
 Please God we find some one to try it on.
 But, truly, would not any one believe
 Some fairy had exchanged us as we lay
 Two tiny foster-children in one cradle?

ROS. Well, be that as it may, Fife, it reminds me
 Of what perhaps I should have thought before,
 But better late than never — You know I love you,
 As you, I know, love me, and loyally
 Have follow'd me thus far in my wild venture.
 Well! now then — having seen me safe thus far
 Safe if not wholly sound — over the rocks
 Into the country where my business lies
 Why should not you return the way we came,
 The storm all clear'd away, and, leaving me
 (Who now shall want you, though not thank you, less,
 Now that our horses gone) this side the ridge,
 Find your way back to dear old home again;
 While I — Come, come! —
 What, weeping my poor fellow?

FIFE. Leave you here
 Alone — my Lady — Lord! I mean my Lord —
 In a strange country — among savages —
 Oh, now I know — you would be rid of me
 For fear my stumbling speech —

ROS. Oh, no, no, no! —
 I want you with me for a thousand sakes
 To which that is as nothing — I myself
 More apt to let the secret out myself
 Without your help at all — Come, come, cheer up!
 And if you sing again, 'Come weal, come woe,'
 Let it be that; for we will never part
 Until you give the signal.

FIFE. 'Tis a bargain.

ROS. Now to begin, then. 'Follow, follow me,
 'You fairy elves that be.'

FIFE. Ay, and go on —
Something of 'following darkness like a dream,'
For that we're after.

ROS. No, after the sun;
 Trying to catch hold of his glittering skirts
 That hang upon the mountain as he goes.

FIFE. Ah, he's himself past catching — as you spoke
 He heard what you were saying, and — just so —
 Like some scared water-bird,
 As we say in my country, *dove* below.

ROS. Well, we must follow him as best we may.
 Poland is no great country, and, as rich
 In men and means, will but few acres spare
 To lie beneath her barrier mountains bare.
 We cannot, I believe, be very far
 From mankind or their dwellings.

FIFE. Send it so!
 And well provided for man, woman, and beast.
 No, not for beast. Ah, but my heart begins
 To yearn for her —

ROS. Keep close, and keep your feet
 From serving you as hers did.

FIFE. As for beasts,
 If in default of other entertainment,
 We should provide them with ourselves to eat —
 Bears, lions, wolves —

ROS. Oh, never fear.

FIFE. Or else,
  Default of other beasts, beastlier men,
  Cannibals, Anthropophagi, bare Poles
  Who never knew a tailor but by taste.

ROS. Look, look! Unless my fancy misconceive
  With twilight — down among the rocks there, Fife —
  Some human dwelling, surely —
  Or think you but a rock torn from the rocks
  In some convulsion like to-day's, and perch'd
  Quaintly among them in mock-masonry?

FIFE. Most likely that, I doubt.

ROS. No, no — for look!
  A square of darkness opening in it —

FIFE. Oh, I don't half like such openings! —

ROS. Like the loom
  Of night from which she spins her outer gloom —

FIFE. Lord, Madam, pray forbear this tragic vein
  In such a time and place —

ROS. And now again
  Within that square of darkness, look! a light
  That feels its way with hesitating pulse,
  As we do, through the darkness that it drives
  To blacken into deeper night beyond.

FIFE. In which could we follow that light's example,
  As might some English Bardolph with his nose,
  We might defy the sunset — Hark, a chain!

ROS. And now a lamp, a lamp! And now the hand

That carries it.

FIFE. Oh, Lord! that dreadful chain!

ROS. And now the bearer of the lamp; indeed
  As strange as any in Arabian tale,
  So giant-like, and terrible, and grand,
  Spite of the skin he's wrapt in.

FIFE. Why, 'tis his own:
  Oh, 'tis some wild man of the woods; I've heard
  They build and carry torches —

ROS. Never Ape
  Bore such a brow before the heavens as that —
  Chain'd as you say too! —

FIFE. Oh, that dreadful chain!

ROS. And now he sets the lamp down by his side,
  And with one hand clench'd in his tangled hair
  And with a sigh as if his heart would break —

(During this Segismund has entered from the fortress, with a torch.)

SEGISMUND. Once more the storm has roar'd itself away,
  Splitting the crags of God as it retires;
  But sparing still what it should only blast,
  This guilty piece of human handiwork,
  And all that are within it. Oh, how oft,
  How oft, within or here abroad, have I
  Waited, and in the whisper of my heart
  Pray'd for the slanting hand of heaven to strike
  The blow myself I dared not, out of fear
  Of that Hereafter, worse, they say, than here,

Plunged headlong in, but, till dismissal waited,
To wipe at last all sorrow from men's eyes,
And make this heavy dispensation clear.
Thus have I borne till now, and still endure,
Crouching in sullen impotence day by day,
Till some such out-burst of the elements
Like this rouses the sleeping fire within;
And standing thus upon the threshold of
Another night about to close the door
Upon one wretched day to open it
On one yet wretcheder because one more; —
Once more, you savage heavens, I ask of you —
I, looking up to those relentless eyes
That, now the greater lamp is gone below,
Begin to muster in the listening skies;
In all the shining circuits you have gone
About this theatre of human woe,
What greater sorrow have you gazed upon
Than down this narrow chink you witness still;
And which, did you yourselves not fore-devise,
You registered for others to fulfil!

FIFE. This is some Laureate at a birthday ode;
No wonder we went rhyming.

ROS. Hush! And now
See, starting to his feet, he strides about
Far as his tether'd steps —

SEG. And if the chain
You help'd to rivet round me did contract
Since guiltless infancy from guilt in act;
Of what in aspiration or in thought
Guilty, but in resentment of the wrong
That wreaks revenge on wrong I never wrought
By excommunication from the free

Inheritance that all created life,
Beside myself, is born to — from the wings
That range your own immeasurable blue,
Down to the poor, mute, scale-imprison'd things,
That yet are free to wander, glide, and pass
About that under-sapphire, whereinto
Yourselves transfusing you yourselves englass!

ROS. What mystery is this?

FIFE. Why, the man's mad:
That's all the mystery. That's why he's chain'd —
And why —

SEG. Nor Nature's guiltless life alone —
But that which lives on blood and rapine; nay,
Charter'd with larger liberty to slay
Their guiltless kind, the tyrants of the air
Soar zenith-upward with their screaming prey,
Making pure heaven drop blood upon the stage
Of under earth, where lion, wolf, and bear,
And they that on their treacherous velvet wear
Figure and constellation like your own,
With their still living slaughter bound away
Over the barriers of the mountain cage,
Against which one, blood-guiltless, and endued
With aspiration and with aptitude
Transcending other creatures, day by day
Beats himself mad with unavailing rage!

FIFE. Why, that must be the meaning of my mule's
Rebellion —

ROS. Hush!

SEG. But then if murder be

The law by which not only conscience-blind
Creatures, but man too prospers with his kind;
Who leaving all his guilty fellows free,
Under your fatal auspice and divine
Compulsion, leagued in some mysterious ban
Against one innocent and helpless man,
Abuse their liberty to murder mine:
And sworn to silence, like their masters mute
In heaven, and like them twirling through the mask
Of darkness, answering to all I ask,
Point up to them whose work they execute!

ROS. Ev'n as I thought, some poor unhappy wretch,
By man wrong'd, wretched, unrevenged, as I!
Nay, so much worse than I, as by those chains
Clipt of the means of self-revenge on those
Who lay on him what they deserve. And I,
Who taunted Heaven a little while ago
With pouring all its wrath upon my head —
Alas! like him who caught the cast-off husk
Of what another bragg'd of feeding on,
Here's one that from the refuse of my sorrows
Could gather all the banquet he desires!
Poor soul, poor soul!

FIFE. Speak lower — he will hear you.

ROS. And if he should, what then? Why, if he would,
He could not harm me — Nay, and if he could,
Methinks I'd venture something of a life
I care so little for —

SEG. Who's that? Clotaldo? Who are you, I say,
That, venturing in these forbidden rocks,
Have lighted on my miserable life,
And your own death?

ROS. You would not hurt me, surely?

SEG. Not I; but those that, iron as the chain
 In which they slay me with a lingering death,
 Will slay you with a sudden — Who are you?

ROS. A stranger from across the mountain there,
 Who, having lost his way in this strange land
 And coming night, drew hither to what seem'd
 A human dwelling hidden in these rocks,
 And where the voice of human sorrow soon
 Told him it was so.

SEG. Ay? But nearer — nearer —
 That by this smoky supplement of day
 But for a moment I may see who speaks
 So pitifully sweet.

FIFE. Take care! take care!

ROS. Alas, poor man, that I, myself so helpless,
 Could better help you than by barren pity,
 And my poor presence —

SEG. Oh, might that be all!
 But that — a few poor moments — and, alas!
 The very bliss of having, and the dread
 Of losing, under such a penalty
 As every moment's having runs more near,
 Stifles the very utterance and resource
 They cry for quickest; till from sheer despair
 Of holding thee, methinks myself would tear
 To pieces —

FIFE. There, his word's enough for it.

SEG. Oh, think, if you who move about at will,
And live in sweet communion with your kind,
After an hour lost in these lonely rocks
Hunger and thirst after some human voice
To drink, and human face to feed upon;
What must one do where all is mute, or harsh,
And ev'n the naked face of cruelty
Were better than the mask it works beneath? —
Across the mountain then! Across the mountain!
What if the next world which they tell one of
Be only next across the mountain then,
Though I must never see it till I die,
And you one of its angels?

ROS. Alas; alas!
No angel! And the face you think so fair,
'Tis but the dismal frame-work of these rocks
That makes it seem so; and the world I come from —
Alas, alas, too many faces there
Are but fair vizors to black hearts below,
Or only serve to bring the wearer woe!
But to yourself — If haply the redress
That I am here upon may help to yours.
I heard you tax the heavens with ordering,
And men for executing, what, alas!
I now behold. But why, and who they are
Who do, and you who suffer —

SEG. (pointing upwards). Ask of them,
Whom, as to-night, I have so often ask'd,
And ask'd in vain.

ROS. But surely, surely —

SEG. Hark!

The trumpet of the watch to shut us in.
Oh, should they find you! — Quick! Behind the rocks!
To-morrow — if to-morrow —

ROS. (flinging her sword toward him). Take my sword!

(Rosaura and Fife hide in the rocks; Enter Clotaldo)

CLOTALDO. These stormy days you like to see the last of
Are but ill opiates, Segismund, I think,
For night to follow: and to-night you seem
More than your wont disorder'd. What! A sword?
Within there!

(Enter Soldiers with black vizors and torches)

FIFE. Here's a pleasant masquerade!

CLO. Whosoever watch this was
Will have to pay head-reckoning. Meanwhile,
This weapon had a wearer. Bring him here,
Alive or dead.

SEG. Clotaldo! good Clotaldo! —

CLO. (to Soldiers who enclose Segismund; others searching the rocks). You know your duty.

SOLDIERS (bringing in Rosaura and Fife). Here are two of them,
Whoever more to follow —

CLO. Who are you,
That in defiance of known proclamation
Are found, at night-fall too, about this place?

FIFE. Oh, my Lord, she — I mean he —

ROS. Silence, Fife,
And let me speak for both. — Two foreign men,
To whom your country and its proclamations
Are equally unknown; and had we known,
Ourselves not masters of our lawless beasts
That, terrified by the storm among your rocks,
Flung us upon them to our cost.

FIFE. My mule —

CLO. Foreigners? Of what country?

ROS. Muscovy.

CLO. And whither bound?

ROS. Hither — if this be Poland;
But with no ill design on her, and therefore
Taking it ill that we should thus be stopt
Upon her threshold so uncivilly.

CLO. Whither in Poland?

ROS. To the capital.

CLO. And on what errand?

ROS. Set me on the road,
And you shall be the nearer to my answer.

CLO. (aside). So resolute and ready to reply,
And yet so young — and —
(Aloud.)
Well, —

Your business was not surely with the man
We found you with?

ROS. He was the first we saw, —
And strangers and benighted, as we were,
As you too would have done in a like case,
Accosted him at once.

CLO. Ay, but this sword?

ROS. I flung it toward him.

CLO. Well, and why?

ROS. And why? But to revenge himself on those who thus
Injuriously misuse him.

CLO. So — so — so!
'Tis well such resolution wants a beard
And, I suppose, is never to attain one.
Well, I must take you both, you and your sword,
Prisoners.

FIFE. (offering a cudgel). Pray take mine, and welcome, sir;
I'm sure I gave it to that mule of mine
To mighty little purpose.

ROS. Mine you have;
And may it win us some more kindliness
Than we have met with yet.

CLO (examining the sword). More mystery!
How came you by this weapon?

ROS. From my father.

CLO. And do you know whence he?

ROS. Oh, very well:
From one of this same Polish realm of yours,
Who promised a return, should come the chance,
Of courtesies that he received himself
In Muscovy, and left this pledge of it —
Not likely yet, it seems, to be redeem'd.

CLO (aside). Oh, wondrous chance — or wondrous Providence!
The sword that I myself in Muscovy,
When these white hairs were black, for keepsake left
Of obligation for a like return
To him who saved me wounded as I lay
Fighting against his country; took me home;
Tended me like a brother till recover'd,
Perchance to fight against him once again
And now my sword put back into my hand
By his — if not his son — still, as so seeming,
By me, as first devoir of gratitude,
To seem believing, till the wearer's self
See fit to drop the ill-dissembling mask.
(Aloud.)
Well, a strange turn of fortune has arrested
The sharp and sudden penalty that else
Had visited your rashness or mischance:
In part, your tender youth too — pardon me,
And touch not where your sword is not to answer —
Commends you to my care; not your life only,
Else by this misadventure forfeited;
But ev'n your errand, which, by happy chance,
Chimes with the very business I am on,
And calls me to the very point you aim at.

ROS. The capital?

CLO. Ay, the capital; and ev'n
That capital of capitals, the Court:
Where you may plead, and, I may promise, win
Pardon for this, you say unwilling, trespass,
And prosecute what else you have at heart,
With me to help you forward all I can;
Provided all in loyalty to those
To whom by natural allegiance
I first am bound to.

ROS. As you make, I take
Your offer: with like promise on my side
Of loyalty to you and those you serve,
Under like reservation for regards
Nearer and dearer still.

CLO. Enough, enough;
Your hand; a bargain on both sides. Meanwhile,
Here shall you rest to-night. The break of day
Shall see us both together on the way.

ROS. Thus then what I for misadventure blamed,
Directly draws me where my wishes aim'd.

(Exeunt.)

## SCENE II

The Palace at Warsaw

Enter on one side Astolfo, Duke of Muscovy, with his train: and, on the
other, the Princess Estrella, with hers.

ASTOLFO.
My royal cousin, if so near in blood,

Till this auspicious meeting scarcely known,
Till all that beauty promised in the bud
Is now to its consummate blossom blown,
Well met at last; and may —

ESTRELLA.
Enough, my Lord,
Of compliment devised for you by some
Court tailor, and, believe me, still too short
To cover the designful heart below.

AST. Nay, but indeed, fair cousin —

EST.
Ay, let Deed
Measure your words, indeed your flowers of speech
Ill with your iron equipage atone;
Irony indeed, and wordy compliment.

AST. Indeed, indeed, you wrong me, royal cousin,
And fair as royal, misinterpreting
What, even for the end you think I aim at,
If false to you, were fatal to myself.

EST.
Why, what else means the glittering steel, my Lord,
That bristles in the rear of these fine words?
What can it mean, but, failing to cajole,
To fight or force me from my just pretension?

AST. Nay, might I not ask ev'n the same of you,
The nodding helmets of whose men-at-arms
Out-crest the plumage of your lady court?

EST.
But to defend what yours would force from me.

AST. Might not I, lady, say the same of mine?
But not to come to battle, ev'n of words,
With a fair lady, and my kinswoman;
And as averse to stand before your face,
Defenceless, and condemn'd in your disgrace,
Till the good king be here to clear it all —
Will you vouchsafe to hear me?

EST.
As you will.

AST. You know that, when about to leave this world,
Our royal grandsire, King Alfonso, left
Three children; one a son, Basilio,
Who wears — long may he wear! the crown of Poland;
And daughters twain: of whom the elder was
Your mother, Clorilena, now some while
Exalted to a more than mortal throne;
And Recisunda, mine, the younger sister,
Who, married to the Prince of Muscovy,
Gave me the light which may she live to see
Herself for many, many years to come.
Meanwhile, good King Basilio, as you know,
Deep in abstruser studies than this world,
And busier with the stars than lady's eyes,
Has never by a second marriage yet
Replaced, as Poland ask'd of him, the heir
An early marriage brought and took away;
His young queen dying with the son she bore him;
And in such alienation grown so old
As leaves no other hope of heir to Poland
Than his two sisters' children; you, fair cousin,
And me; for whom the Commons of the realm
Divide themselves into two several factions;
Whether for you, the elder sister's child;

Or me, born of the younger, but, they say,
My natural prerogative of man
Outweighing your priority of birth.
Which discord growing loud and dangerous,
Our uncle, King Basilio, doubly sage
In prophesying and providing for
The future, as to deal with it when come,
Bids us here meet to-day in solemn council
Our several pretensions to compose.
And, but the martial out-burst that proclaims
His coming, makes all further parley vain,
Unless my bosom, by which only wise
I prophesy, now wrongly prophesies,
By such a happy compact as I dare
But glance at till the Royal Sage declare.

(Trumpets, etc. Enter King Basilio with his Council.)

ALL.
 The King! God save the King!

ESTRELLA (Kneeling.)
 Oh, Royal Sir! —

ASTOLFO (Kneeling.)
 God save your Majesty —

KING. Rise both of you,
 Rise to my arms, Astolfo and Estrella;
 As my two sisters' children always mine,
 Now more than ever, since myself and Poland
 Solely to you for our succession look'd.
 And now give ear, you and your several factions,
 And you, the Peers and Princes of this realm,
 While I reveal the purport of this meeting
 In words whose necessary length I trust

No unsuccessful issue shall excuse.
You and the world who have surnamed me "Sage"
Know that I owe that title, if my due,
To my long meditation on the book
Which ever lying open overhead —
The book of heaven, I mean — so few have read;
Whose golden letters on whose sapphire leaf,
Distinguishing the page of day and night,
And all the revolution of the year;
So with the turning volume where they lie
Still changing their prophetic syllables,
They register the destinies of men:
Until with eyes that, dim with years indeed,
Are quicker to pursue the stars than rule them,
I get the start of Time, and from his hand
The wand of tardy revelation draw.
Oh, had the self-same heaven upon his page
Inscribed my death ere I should read my life
And, by fore-casting of my own mischance,
Play not the victim but the suicide
In my own tragedy! — But you shall hear.
You know how once, as kings must for their people,
And only once, as wise men for themselves,
I woo'd and wedded: know too that my Queen
In childing died; but not, as you believe,
With her, the son she died in giving life to.
For, as the hour of birth was on the stroke,
Her brain conceiving with her womb, she dream'd
A serpent tore her entrail. And too surely
(For evil omen seldom speaks in vain)
The man-child breaking from that living tomb
That makes our birth the antitype of death,
Man-grateful, for the life she gave him paid
By killing her: and with such circumstance
As suited such unnatural tragedy;
He coming into light, if light it were

That darken'd at his very horoscope,
When heaven's two champions — sun and moon I mean —
Suffused in blood upon each other fell
In such a raging duel of eclipse
As hath not terrified the universe
Since that which wept in blood the death of Christ:
When the dead walk'd, the waters turn'd to blood,
Earth and her cities totter'd, and the world
Seem'd shaken to its last paralysis.
In such a paroxysm of dissolution
That son of mine was born; by that first act
Heading the monstrous catalogue of crime,
I found fore-written in his horoscope;
As great a monster in man's history
As was in nature his nativity;
So savage, bloody, terrible, and impious,
Who, should he live, would tear his country's entrails,
As by his birth his mother's; with which crime
Beginning, he should clench the dreadful tale
By trampling on his father's silver head.
All which fore-reading, and his act of birth
Fate's warrant that I read his life aright;
To save his country from his mother's fate,
I gave abroad that he had died with her
His being slew; with midnight secrecy
I had him carried to a lonely tower
Hewn from the mountain-barriers of the realm,
And under strict anathema of death
Guarded from men's inquisitive approach,
Save from the trusty few one needs must trust;
Who while his fasten'd body they provide
With salutary garb and nourishment,
Instruct his soul in what no soul may miss
Of holy faith, and in such other lore
As may solace his life-imprisonment,
And tame perhaps the Savage prophesied

Toward such a trial as I aim at now,
And now demand your special hearing to.
What in this fearful business I have done,
Judge whether lightly or maliciously, —
I, with my own and only flesh and blood,
And proper lineal inheritor!
I swear, had his foretold atrocities
Touch'd me alone. I had not saved myself
At such a cost to him; but as a king, —
A Christian king, — I say, advisedly,
Who would devote his people to a tyrant
Worse than Caligula fore-chronicled?
But even this not without grave mis-giving,
Lest by some chance mis-reading of the stars,
Or mis-direction of what rightly read,
I wrong my son of his prerogative,
And Poland of her rightful sovereign.
For, sure and certain prophets as the stars,
Although they err not, he who reads them may;
Or rightly reading — seeing there is One
Who governs them, as, under Him, they us,
We are not sure if the rough diagram
They draw in heaven and we interpret here,
Be sure of operation, if the Will
Supreme, that sometimes for some special end
The course of providential nature breaks
By miracle, may not of these same stars
Cancel his own first draft, or overrule
What else fore-written all else overrules.
As, for example, should the Will Almighty
Permit the Free-will of particular man
To break the meshes of else strangling fate —
Which Free-will, fearful of foretold abuse,
I have myself from my own son fore-closed
From ever possible self-extrication;
A terrible responsibility,

Not to the conscience to be reconciled
Unless opposing almost certain evil
Against so slight contingency of good.
Well — thus perplex'd, I have resolved at last
To bring the thing to trial: whereunto
Here have I summon'd you, my Peers, and you
Whom I more dearly look to, failing him,
As witnesses to that which I propose;
And thus propose the doing it. Clotaldo,
Who guards my son with old fidelity,
Shall bring him hither from his tower by night
Lockt in a sleep so fast as by my art
I rivet to within a link of death,
But yet from death so far, that next day's dawn
Shall wake him up upon the royal bed,
Complete in consciousness and faculty,
When with all princely pomp and retinue
My loyal Peers with due obeisance
Shall hail him Segismund, the Prince of Poland.
Then if with any show of human kindness
He fling discredit, not upon the stars,
But upon me, their misinterpreter,
With all apology mistaken age
Can make to youth it never meant to harm,
To my son's forehead will I shift the crown
I long have wish'd upon a younger brow;
And in religious humiliation,
For what of worn-out age remains to me,
Entreat my pardon both of Heaven and him
For tempting destinies beyond my reach.
But if, as I misdoubt, at his first step
The hoof of the predicted savage shows;
Before predicted mischief can be done,
The self-same sleep that loosed him from the chain
Shall re-consign him, not to loose again.
Then shall I, having lost that heir direct,

Look solely to my sisters' children twain
Each of a claim so equal as divides
The voice of Poland to their several sides,
But, as I trust, to be entwined ere long
Into one single wreath so fair and strong
As shall at once all difference atone,
And cease the realm's division with their own.
Cousins and Princes, Peers and Councillors,
Such is the purport of this invitation,
And such is my design. Whose furtherance
If not as Sovereign, if not as Seer,
Yet one whom these white locks, if nothing else,
to patient acquiescence consecrate,
I now demand and even supplicate.

AST. Such news, and from such lips, may well suspend
The tongue to loyal answer most attuned;
But if to me as spokesman of my faction
Your Highness looks for answer; I reply
For one and all — Let Segismund, whom now
We first hear tell of as your living heir,
Appear, and but in your sufficient eye
Approve himself worthy to be your son,
Then we will hail him Poland's rightful heir.
What says my cousin?

EST.
Ay, with all my heart.
But if my youth and sex upbraid me not
That I should dare ask of so wise a king —

KING. Ask, ask, fair cousin! Nothing, I am sure,
Not well consider'd; nay, if 'twere, yet nothing
But pardonable from such lips as those.

EST.

Then, with your pardon, Sir — if Segismund,
My cousin, whom I shall rejoice to hail
As Prince of Poland too, as you propose,
Be to a trial coming upon which
More, as I think, than life itself depends,
Why, Sir, with sleep-disorder'd senses brought
To this uncertain contest with his stars?

KING. Well ask'd indeed! As wisely be it answer'd!
*Because* it is uncertain, see you not?
For as I think I can discern between
The sudden flaws of a sleep-startled man,
And of the savage thing we have to dread;
If but bewilder'd, dazzled, and uncouth,
As might the sanest and the civilest
In circumstance so strange — nay, more than that,
If moved to any out-break short of blood,
All shall be well with him; and how much more,
If 'mid the magic turmoil of the change,
He shall so calm a resolution show
As scarce to reel beneath so great a blow!
But if with savage passion uncontroll'd
He lay about him like the brute foretold,
And must as suddenly be caged again;
Then what redoubled anguish and despair,
From that brief flash of blissful liberty
Remitted — and for ever — to his chain!
Which so much less, if on the stage of glory
Enter'd and exited through such a door
Of sleep as makes a dream of all between.

EST.
Oh kindly answer, Sir, to question that
To charitable courtesy less wise
Might call for pardon rather! I shall now
Gladly, what, uninstructed, loyally

I should have waited.

AST. Your Highness doubts not me,
Nor how my heart follows my cousin's lips,
Whatever way the doubtful balance fall,
Still loyal to your bidding.

OMNES.
So say all.

KING. I hoped, and did expect, of all no less —
And sure no sovereign ever needed more
From all who owe him love or loyalty.
For what a strait of time I stand upon,
When to this issue not alone I bring
My son your Prince, but e'en myself your King:
And, whichsoever way for him it turn,
Of less than little honour to myself.
For if this coming trial justify
My thus withholding from my son his right,
Is not the judge himself justified in
The father's shame? And if the judge proved wrong,
My son withholding from his right thus long,
Shame and remorse to judge and father both:
Unless remorse and shame together drown'd
In having what I flung for worthless found.
But come — already weary with your travel,
And ill refresh'd by this strange history,
Until the hours that draw the sun from heaven
Unite us at the customary board,
Each to his several chamber: you to rest;
I to contrive with old Clotaldo best
The method of a stranger thing than old
Time has a yet among his records told.

Exeunt.

## ACT THE SECOND

### SCENE I

A Throne-room in the Palace. Music within.

(Enter King and Clotaldo, meeting a Lord in waiting)

KING. You, for a moment beckon'd from your office,
Tell me thus far how goes it. In due time
The potion left him?

LORD.
At the very hour
To which your Highness temper'd it. Yet not
So wholly but some lingering mist still hung
About his dawning senses — which to clear,
We fill'd and handed him a morning drink
With sleep's specific antidote suffused;
And while with princely raiment we invested
What nature surely modell'd for a Prince —
All but the sword — as you directed —

KING. Ay —

LORD.
If not too loudly, yet emphatically
Still with the title of a Prince address'd him.

KING. How bore he that?

LORD.
With all the rest, my liege,
I will not say so like one in a dream
As one himself misdoubting that he dream'd.

KING. So far so well, Clotaldo, either way,
And best of all if tow'rd the worse I dread.
But yet no violence?

LORD.
At most, impatience;
Wearied perhaps with importunities
We yet were bound to offer.

KING. Oh, Clotaldo!
Though thus far well, yet would myself had drunk
The potion he revives from! such suspense
Crowds all the pulses of life's residue
Into the present moment; and, I think,
Whichever way the trembling scale may turn,
Will leave the crown of Poland for some one
To wait no longer than the setting sun!

CLO. Courage, my liege! The curtain is undrawn,
And each must play his part out manfully,
Leaving the rest to heaven.

KING. Whose written words
If I should misinterpret or transgress!
But as you say —
(To the Lord, who exit.)
You, back to him at once;
Clotaldo, you, when he is somewhat used
To the new world of which they call him Prince,
Where place and face, and all, is strange to him,
With your known features and familiar garb
Shall then, as chorus to the scene, accost him,
And by such earnest of that old and too
Familiar world, assure him of the new.
Last in the strange procession, I myself

Will by one full and last development
Complete the plot for that catastrophe
That he must put to all; God grant it be
The crown of Poland on his brows! — Hark! hark! —
Was that his voice within! — Now louder — Oh,
Clotaldo, what! so soon begun to roar! —
Again! above the music — But betide
What may, until the moment, we must hide.

(Exeunt King and Clotaldo.)

SEGISMUND (within). Forbear! I stifle with your perfume!
Cease
 Your crazy salutations! peace, I say
Begone, or let me go, ere I go mad
With all this babble, mummery, and glare,
For I am growing dangerous — Air! room! air! —
(He rushes in. Music ceases.)
Oh but to save the reeling brain from wreck
With its bewilder'd senses!
(He covers his eyes for a while.)
What! E'en now
That Babel left behind me, but my eyes
Pursued by the same glamour, that — unless
Alike bewitch'd too — the confederate sense
Vouches for palpable: bright-shining floors
That ring hard answer back to the stamp'd heel,
And shoot up airy columns marble-cold,
That, as they climb, break into golden leaf
And capital, till they embrace aloft
In clustering flower and fruitage over walls
Hung with such purple curtain as the West
Fringes with such a gold; or over-laid
With sanguine-glowing semblances of men,
Each in his all but living action busied,
Or from the wall they look from, with fix'd eyes

Pursuing me; and one most strange of all
That, as I pass'd the crystal on the wall,
Look'd from it — left it — and as I return,
Returns, and looks me face to face again —
Unless some false reflection of my brain,
The outward semblance of myself — Myself?
How know that tawdry shadow for myself,
But that it moves as I move; lifts his hand
With mine; each motion echoing so close
The immediate suggestion of the will
In which myself I recognize — Myself! —
What, this fantastic Segismund the same
Who last night, as for all his nights before,
Lay down to sleep in wolf-skin on the ground
In a black turret which the wolf howl'd round,
And woke again upon a golden bed,
Round which as clouds about a rising sun,
In scarce less glittering caparison,
Gather'd gay shapes that, underneath a breeze
Of music, handed him upon their knees
The wine of heaven in a cup of gold,
And still in soft melodious under-song
Hailing me Prince of Poland! — 'Segismund,'
They said, 'Our Prince! The Prince of Poland!' and
Again, 'Oh, welcome, welcome, to his own,
'Our own Prince Segismund — '
Oh, but a blast —
One blast of the rough mountain air! one look
At the grim features —
(He goes to the window.)
What they disvizor'd also! shatter'd chaos
Cast into stately shape and masonry,
Between whose channel'd and perspective sides
Compact with rooted towers, and flourishing
To heaven with gilded pinnacle and spire,
Flows the live current ever to and fro

With open aspect and free step! — Clotaldo!
Clotaldo! — calling as one scarce dares call
For him who suddenly might break the spell
One fears to walk without him — Why, that I,
With unencumber'd step as any there,
Go stumbling through my glory — feeling for
That iron leading-string — ay, for myself —
For that fast-anchor'd self of yesterday,
Of yesterday, and all my life before,
Ere drifted clean from self-identity
Upon the fluctuation of to-day's
Mad whirling circumstance! — And, fool, why not?
If reason, sense, and self-identity
Obliterated from a worn-out brain,
Art thou not maddest striving to be sane,
And catching at that Self of yesterday
That, like a leper's rags, best flung away!
Or if not mad, then dreaming — dreaming? — well —
Dreaming then — Or, if self to self be true,
Not mock'd by that, but as poor souls have been
By those who wrong'd them, to give wrong new relish?
Or have those stars indeed they told me of
As masters of my wretched life of old,
Into some happier constellation roll'd,
And brought my better fortune out on earth
Clear as themselves in heaven! — Prince Segismund
They call'd me — and at will I shook them off —
Will they return again at my command
Again to call me so? — Within there! You!
Segismund calls — Prince Segismund —

(He has seated himself on the throne.
Enter Chamberlain, with lords in waiting.)

CHAMB.
I rejoice

That unadvised of any but the voice
Of royal instinct in the blood, your Highness
Has ta'en the chair that you were born to fill.

SEG. The chair?

CHAMB.
The royal throne of Poland, Sir,
Which may your Royal Highness keep as long
As he that now rules from it shall have ruled
When heaven has call'd him to itself.

SEG. When he? —

CHAMB.
Your royal father, King Basilio, Sir.

SEG. My royal father — King Basilio.
You see I answer but as Echo does,
Not knowing what she listens or repeats.
This is my throne — this is my palace — Oh,
But this out of the window? —

CHAMB.
Warsaw, Sir,
Your capital —

SEG. And all the moving people?

CHAMB.
Your subjects and your vassals like ourselves.

SEG. Ay, ay — my subjects — in my capital —
Warsaw — and I am Prince of it — You see
It needs much iteration to strike sense
Into the human echo.

CHAMB.
Left awhile
In the quick brain, the word will quickly to
Full meaning blow.

SEG. You think so?

CHAMB.
And meanwhile
Lest our obsequiousness, which means no worse
Than customary honour to the Prince
We most rejoice to welcome, trouble you,
Should we retire again? or stand apart?
Or would your Highness have the music play
Again, which meditation, as they say,
So often loves to float upon?

SEG. The music?
No — yes — perhaps the trumpet —
(Aside)
Yet if that
Brought back the troop!

A LORD.
The trumpet! There again
How trumpet-like spoke out the blood of Poland!

CHAMB.
Before the morning is far up, your Highness
Will have the trumpet marshalling your soldiers
Under the Palace windows.

SEG. Ah, my soldiers —
My soldiers — not black-vizor'd? —

CHAMB.
 Sir?

SEG. No matter.
 But — one thing — for a moment — in your ear —
 Do you know one Clotaldo?

CHAMB.
 Oh, my Lord,
 He and myself together, I may say,
 Although in different vocations,
 Have silver'd in your royal father's service;
 And, as I trust, with both of us a few
 White hairs to fall in yours.

SEG. Well said, well said!
 Basilio, my father — well — Clotaldo
 Is he my kinsman too?

CHAMB.
 Oh, my good Lord,
 A General simply in your Highness' service,
 Than whom your Highness has no trustier.

SEG. Ay, so you said before, I think. And you
 With that white wand of yours —
 Why, now I think on't, I have read of such
 A silver-hair'd magician with a wand,
 Who in a moment, with a wave of it,
 Turn'd rags to jewels, clowns to emperors,
 By some benigner magic than the stars
 Spirited poor good people out of hand
 From all their woes; in some enchanted sleep
 Carried them off on cloud or dragon-back
 Over the mountains, over the wide Deep,
 And set them down to wake in Fairyland.

CHAMB.
Oh, my good Lord, you laugh at me — and I
Right glad to make you laugh at such a price:
You know me no enchanter: if I were,
I and my wand as much as your Highness',
As now your chamberlain —

SEG. My chamberlain? —
And these that follow you? —

CHAMB.
On you, my Lord,
Your Highness' lords in waiting.

SEG. Lords in waiting.
Well, I have now learn'd to repeat, I think,
If only but by rote — This is my palace,
And this my throne — which unadvised — And that
Out of the window there my Capital;
And all the people moving up and down
My subjects and my vassals like yourselves,
My chamberlain — and lords in waiting — and
Clotaldo — and Clotaldo? —
You are an aged, and seem a reverend man —
You do not — though his fellow-officer —
You do not mean to mock me?

CHAMB.
Oh, my Lord!

SEG. Well then — If no magician, as you say,
Yet setting me a riddle, that my brain,
With all its senses whirling, cannot solve,
Yourself or one of these with you must answer —
How I — that only last night fell asleep

Not knowing that the very soil of earth
I lay down — chain'd — to sleep upon was Poland —
Awake to find myself the Lord of it,
With Lords, and Generals, and Chamberlains,
And ev'n my very Gaoler, for my vassals!

Enter suddenly Clotaldo

CLOTALDO.
Stand all aside
That I may put into his hand the clue
To lead him out of this amazement. Sir,
Vouchsafe your Highness from my bended knee
Receive my homage first.

SEG. Clotaldo! What,
At last — his old self — undisguised where all
Is masquerade — to end it! — You kneeling too!
What! have the stars you told me long ago
Laid that old work upon you, added this,
That, having chain'd your prisoner so long,
You loose his body now to slay his wits,
Dragging him — how I know not — whither scarce
I understand — dressing him up in all
This frippery, with your dumb familiars
Disvizor'd, and their lips unlock'd to lie,
Calling him Prince and King, and, madman-like,
Setting a crown of straw upon his head?

CLO. Would but your Highness, as indeed I now
Must call you — and upon his bended knee
Never bent Subject more devotedly —
However all about you, and perhaps
You to yourself incomprehensiblest,
But rest in the assurance of your own
Sane waking senses, by these witnesses

Attested, till the story of it all,
Of which I bring a chapter, be reveal'd,
Assured of all you see and hear as neither
Madness nor mockery —

SEG. What then?

CLO. All it seems:
This palace with its royal garniture;
This capital of which it is the eye,
With all its temples, marts, and arsenals;
This realm of which this city is the head,
With all its cities, villages, and tilth,
Its armies, fleets, and commerce; all your own;
And all the living souls that make them up,
From those who now, and those who shall, salute you,
Down to the poorest peasant of the realm,
Your subjects — Who, though now their mighty voice
Sleeps in the general body unapprized,
Wait but a word from those about you now
To hail you Prince of Poland, Segismund.

SEG. All this is so?

CLO. As sure as anything
Is, or can be.

SEG. You swear it on the faith
You taught me — elsewhere? —

CLO (kissing the hilt of his sword). Swear it upon this Symbol,
and champion of the holy faith
I wear it to defend.

SEG (to himself). My eyes have not deceived me, nor my ears,
With this transfiguration, nor the strain

Of royal welcome that arose and blew,
Breathed from no lying lips, along with it.
For here Clotaldo comes, his own old self,
Who, if not Lie and phantom with the rest —
(Aloud)
Well, then, all this is thus.
For have not these fine people told me so,
And you, Clotaldo, sworn it? And the Why
And Wherefore are to follow by and bye!
And yet — and yet — why wait for that which you
Who take your oath on it can answer — and
Indeed it presses hard upon my brain —
What I was asking of these gentlemen
When you came in upon us; how it is
That I — the Segismund you know so long
No longer than the sun that rose to-day
Rose — and from what you know —
Rose to be Prince of Poland?

CLO. So to be
Acknowledged and entreated, Sir.

SEG. So be
Acknowledged and entreated —
Well — But if now by all, by some at least
So known — if not entreated — heretofore —
Though not by you — For, now I think again,
Of what should be your attestation worth,
You that of all my questionable subjects
Who knowing what, yet left me where I was,
You least of all, Clotaldo, till the dawn
Of this first day that told it to myself?

CLO. Oh, let your Highness draw the line across
Fore-written sorrow, and in this new dawn
Bury that long sad night.

SEG. Not ev'n the Dead,
  Call'd to the resurrection of the blest,
  Shall so directly drop all memory
  Of woes and wrongs foregone!

CLO. But not resent —
  Purged by the trial of that sorrow past
  For full fruition of their present bliss.

SEG. But leaving with the Judge what, till this earth
  Be cancell'd in the burning heavens, He leaves
  His earthly delegates to execute,
  Of retribution in reward to them
  And woe to those who wrong'd them — Not as you,
  Not you, Clotaldo, knowing not — And yet
  Ev'n to the guiltiest wretch in all the realm,
  Of any treason guilty short of that,
  Stern usage — but assuredly not knowing,
  Not knowing 'twas your sovereign lord, Clotaldo,
  You used so sternly.

CLO. Ay, sir; with the same
  Devotion and fidelity that now
  Does homage to him for my sovereign.

SEG. Fidelity that held his Prince in chains!

CLO. Fidelity more fast than had it loosed him —

SEG. Ev'n from the very dawn of consciousness
  Down at the bottom of the barren rocks,
  Where scarce a ray of sunshine found him out,
  In which the poorest beggar of my realm
  At least to human-full proportion grows —
  Me! Me — whose station was the kingdom's top

To flourish in, reaching my head to heaven,
And with my branches overshadowing
The meaner growth below!

CLO. Still with the same
Fidelity —

SEG. To me! —

CLO. Ay, sir, to you,
Through that divine allegiance upon which
All Order and Authority is based;
Which to revolt against —

SEG. Were to revolt
Against the stars, belike!

CLO. And him who reads them;
And by that right, and by the sovereignty
He wears as you shall wear it after him;
Ay, one to whom yourself —
Yourself, ev'n more than any subject here,
Are bound by yet another and more strong
Allegiance — King Basilio — your Father —

SEG. Basilio — King — my father! —

CLO. Oh, my Lord,
Let me beseech you on my bended knee,
For your own sake — for Poland's — and for his,
Who, looking up for counsel to the skies,
Did what he did under authority
To which the kings of earth themselves are subject,
And whose behest not only he that suffers,
But he that executes, not comprehends,
But only He that orders it —

SEG. The King —
My father! — Either I am mad already,
Or that way driving fast — or I should know
That fathers do not use their children so,
Or men were loosed from all allegiance
To fathers, kings, and heaven that order'd all.
But, mad or not, my hour is come, and I
Will have my reckoning — Either you lie,
Under the skirt of sinless majesty
Shrouding your treason; or if *that* indeed,
Guilty itself, take refuge in the stars
That cannot hear the charge, or disavow —
You, whether doer or deviser, who
Come first to hand, shall pay the penalty
By the same hand you owe it to —
(Seizing Clotaldo's sword and about to strike him.)

(Enter Rosaura suddenly.)

ROSAURA.
Fie, my Lord — forbear,
What! a young hand raised against silver hair! —

(She retreats through the crowd.)

SEG. Stay! stay! What come and vanish'd as before —
I scarce remember how — but —

(Voices within. Room for Astolfo, Duke of Muscovy!)

(Enter Astolfo)

ASTOLFO.
Welcome, thrice welcome, the auspicious day,
When from the mountain where he darkling lay,

The Polish sun into the firmament
Sprung all the brighter for his late ascent,
And in meridian glory —

SEG. Where is he?
Why must I ask this twice? —

A LORD.
The Page, my Lord?
I wonder at his boldness —

SEG. But I tell you
He came with Angel written in his face
As now it is, when all was black as hell
About, and none of you who now — he came,
And Angel-like flung me a shining sword
To cut my way through darkness; and again
Angel-like wrests it from me in behalf
Of one — whom I will spare for sparing him:
But he must come and plead with that same voice
That pray'd for me — in vain.

CHAMB.
He is gone for,
And shall attend your pleasure, sir. Meanwhile,
Will not your Highness, as in courtesy,
Return your royal cousin's greeting?

SEG. Whose?

CHAMB.
Astolfo, Duke of Muscovy, my Lord,
Saluted, and with gallant compliment
Welcomed you to your royal title.

SEG. (to Astolfo). Oh —

You knew of this then?

AST. Knew of what, my Lord?

SEG. That I was Prince of Poland all the while,
And you my subject?

AST. Pardon me, my Lord,
But some few hours ago myself I learn'd
Your dignity; but, knowing it, no more
Than when I knew it not, your subject.

SEG. What then?

AST. Your Highness' chamberlain ev'n now has told you;
Astolfo, Duke of Muscovy,
Your father's sister's son; your cousin, sir:
And who as such, and in his own right Prince,
Expects from you the courtesy he shows.

CHAMB.
His Highness is as yet unused to Court,
And to the ceremonious interchange
Of compliment, especially to those
Who draw their blood from the same royal fountain.

SEG. Where is the lad? I weary of all this —
Prince, cousins, chamberlains, and compliments —
Where are my soldiers? Blow the trumpet, and
With one sharp blast scatter these butterflies
And bring the men of iron to my side,
With whom a king feels like a king indeed!

(Voices within. Within there! room for the Princess Estrella!)

(Enter Estrella with Ladies.)

ESTRELLA.
 Welcome, my Lord, right welcome to the throne
 That much too long has waited for your coming:
 And, in the general voice of Poland, hear
 A kinswoman and cousin's no less sincere.

SEG. Ay, this is welcome-worth indeed,
 And cousin cousin-worth! Oh, I have thus
 Over the threshold of the mountain seen,
 Leading a bevy of fair stars, the moon
 Enter the court of heaven — My kinswoman!
 My cousin! But my subject? —

EST.
 If you please
 To count your cousin for your subject, sir,
 You shall not find her a disloyal.

SEG. Oh,
 But there are twin stars in that heavenly face,
 That now I know for having over-ruled
 Those evil ones that darken'd all my past
 And brought me forth from that captivity
 To be the slave of her who set me free.

EST.
 Indeed, my Lord, these eyes have no such power
 Over the past or present: but perhaps
 They brighten at your welcome to supply
 The little that a lady's speech commends;
 And in the hope that, let whichever be
 The other's subject, we may both be friends.

SEG. Your hand to that — But why does this warm hand
 Shoot a cold shudder through me?

EST.
In revenge
For likening me to that cold moon, perhaps.

SEG. Oh, but the lip whose music tells me so
Breathes of a warmer planet, and that lip
Shall remedy the treason of the hand!
(He catches to embrace her.)

EST.
Release me, sir!

CHAMB.
And pardon me, my Lord.
This lady is a Princess absolute,
As Prince he is who just saluted you,
And claims her by affiance.

SEG. Hence, old fool,
For ever thrusting that white stick of yours
Between me and my pleasure!

AST. This cause is mine.
Forbear, sir —

SEG. What, sir mouth-piece, you again?

AST. My Lord, I waive your insult to myself
In recognition of the dignity
You yet are new to, and that greater still
You look in time to wear. But for this lady —
Whom, if my cousin now, I hope to claim
Henceforth by yet a nearer, dearer name —

SEG. And what care I? She is my cousin too:

And if you be a Prince — well, am not I
Lord of the very soil you stand upon?
By that, and by that right beside of blood
That like a fiery fountain hitherto
Pent in the rock leaps toward her at her touch,
Mine, before all the cousins in Muscovy!
You call me Prince of Poland, and yourselves
My subjects — traitors therefore to this hour,
Who let me perish all my youth away
Chain'd there among the mountains; till, forsooth,
Terrified at your treachery foregone,
You spirit me up here, I know not how,
Popinjay-like invest me like yourselves,
Choke me with scent and music that I loathe,
And, worse than all the music and the scent,
With false, long-winded, fulsome compliment,
That 'Oh, you are my subjects!' and in word
Reiterating still obedience,
Thwart me in deed at every step I take:
When just about to wreak a just revenge
Upon that old arch-traitor of you all,
Filch from my vengeance him I hate; and him
I loved — the first and only face — till this —
I cared to look on in your ugly court —
And now when palpably I grasp at last
What hitherto but shadow'd in my dreams —
Affiances and interferences,
The first who dares to meddle with me more —
Princes and chamberlains and counsellors,
Touch her who dares! —

AST. That dare I —

SEG. (seizing him by the throat). You dare!

CHAMB.

My Lord! —

A LORD.
His strength's a lion's —

(Voices within. The King! The King! — )

(Enter King.)

A LORD.
And on a sudden how he stands at gaze
As might a wolf just fasten'd on his prey,
Glaring at a suddenly encounter'd lion.

KING. And I that hither flew with open arms
To fold them round my son, must now return
To press them to an empty heart again!
(He sits on the throne.)

SEG. That is the King? — My father?
(After a long pause.)
I have heard
That sometimes some blind instinct has been known
To draw to mutual recognition those
Of the same blood, beyond all memory
Divided, or ev'n never met before.
I know not how this is — perhaps in brutes
That live by kindlier instincts — but I know
That looking now upon that head whose crown
Pronounces him a sovereign king, I feel
No setting of the current in my blood
Tow'rd him as sire. How is't with you, old man,
Tow'rd him they call your son? —

KING. Alas! Alas!

SEG. Your sorrow, then?

KING. Beholding what I do.

SEG. Ay, but how know this sorrow that has grown
And moulded to this present shape of man,
As of your own creation?

KING. Ev'n from birth.

SEG. But from that hour to this, near, as I think,
Some twenty such renewals of the year
As trace themselves upon the barren rocks,
I never saw you, nor you me — unless,
Unless, indeed, through one of those dark masks
Through which a son might fail to recognize
The best of fathers.

KING. Be that as you will:
But, now we see each other face to face,
Know me as you I know; which did I not,
By whatsoever signs, assuredly
You were not here to prove it at my risk.

SEG. You are my father.
And is it true then, as Clotaldo swears,
'Twas you that from the dawning birth of one
Yourself brought into being, — you, I say,
Who stole his very birthright; not alone
That secondary and peculiar right
Of sovereignty, but even that prime
Inheritance that all men share alike,
And chain'd him — chain'd him! — like a wild beast's whelp.
Among as savage mountains, to this hour?
Answer if this be thus.

KING. Oh, Segismund,
  In all that I have done that seems to you,
  And, without further hearing, fairly seems,
  Unnatural and cruel — 'twas not I,
  But One who writes His order in the sky
  I dared not misinterpret nor neglect,
  Who knows with what reluctance —

SEG. Oh, those stars,
  Those stars, that too far up from human blame
  To clear themselves, or careless of the charge,
  Still bear upon their shining shoulders all
  The guilt men shift upon them!

KING. Nay, but think:
  Not only on the common score of kind,
  But that peculiar count of sovereignty —
  If not behind the beast in brain as heart,
  How should I thus deal with my innocent child,
  Doubly desired, and doubly dear when come,
  As that sweet second-self that all desire,
  And princes more than all, to root themselves
  By that succession in their people's hearts,
  Unless at that superior Will, to which
  Not kings alone, but sovereign nature bows?

SEG. And what had those same stars to tell of me
  That should compel a father and a king
  So much against that double instinct?

KING. That,
  Which I have brought you hither, at my peril,
  Against their written warning, to disprove,
  By justice, mercy, human kindliness.

SEG. And therefore made yourself their instrument

To make your son the savage and the brute
   They only prophesied? — Are you not afear'd,
   Lest, irrespective as such creatures are
   Of such relationship, the brute you made
   Revenge the man you marr'd — like sire, like son.
   To do by you as you by me have done?

KING. You never had a savage heart from me;
   I may appeal to Poland.

SEG. Then from whom?
   If pure in fountain, poison'd by yourself
   When scarce begun to flow. — To make a man
   Not, as I see, degraded from the mould
   I came from, nor compared to those about,
   And then to throw your own flesh to the dogs! —
   Why not at once, I say, if terrified
   At the prophetic omens of my birth,
   Have drown'd or stifled me, as they do whelps
   Too costly or too dangerous to keep?

KING. That, living, you might learn to live, and rule
   Yourself and Poland.

SEG. By the means you took
   To spoil for either?

KING. Nay, but, Segismund!
   You know not — cannot know — happily wanting
   The sad experience on which knowledge grows,
   How the too early consciousness of power
   Spoils the best blood; nor whether for your long
   Constrain'd disheritance (which, but for me,
   Remember, and for my relenting love
   Bursting the bond of fate, had been eternal)
   You have not now a full indemnity;

Wearing the blossom of your youth unspent
In the voluptuous sunshine of a court,
That often, by too early blossoming,
Too soon deflowers the rose of royalty.

SEG. Ay, but what some precocious warmth may spill,
May not an early frost as surely kill?

KING. But, Segismund, my son, whose quick discourse
Proves I have not extinguish'd and destroy'd
The Man you charge me with extinguishing,
However it condemn me for the fault
Of keeping a good light so long eclipsed,
Reflect! This is the moment upon which
Those stars, whose eyes, although we see them not,
By day as well as night are on us still,
Hang watching up in the meridian heaven
Which way the balance turns; and if to you —
As by your dealing God decide it may,
To my confusion! — let me answer it
Unto yourself alone, who shall at once
Approve yourself to be your father's judge,
And sovereign of Poland in his stead,
By justice, mercy, self-sobriety,
And all the reasonable attributes
Without which, impotent to rule himself,
Others one cannot, and one must not rule;
But which if you but show the blossom of —
All that is past we shall but look upon
As the first out-fling of a generous nature
Rioting in first liberty; and if
This blossom do but promise such a flower
As promises in turn its kindly fruit:
Forthwith upon your brows the royal crown,
That now weighs heavy on my aged brows,
I will devolve; and while I pass away

Into some cloister, with my Maker there
To make my peace in penitence and prayer,
Happily settle the disorder'd realm
That now cries loudly for a lineal heir.

SEG. And so —
When the crown falters on your shaking head,
And slips the sceptre from your palsied hand,
And Poland for her rightful heir cries out;
When not only your stol'n monopoly
Fails you of earthly power, but 'cross the grave
The judgment-trumpet of another world
Calls you to count for your abuse of this;
Then, oh then, terrified by the double danger,
You drag me from my den —
Boast not of giving up at last the power
You can no longer hold, and never rightly
Held, but in fee for him you robb'd it from;
And be assured your Savage, once let loose,
Will not be caged again so quickly; not
By threat or adulation to be tamed,
Till he have had his quarrel out with those
Who made him what he is.

KING. Beware! Beware!
Subdue the kindled Tiger in your eye,
Nor dream that it was sheer necessity
Made me thus far relax the bond of fate,
And, with far more of terror than of hope
Threaten myself, my people, and the State.
Know that, if old, I yet have vigour left
To wield the sword as well as wear the crown;
And if my more immediate issue fail,
Not wanting scions of collateral blood,
Whose wholesome growth shall more than compensate
For all the loss of a distorted stem.

SEG. That will I straightway bring to trial — Oh,
After a revelation such as this,
The Last Day shall have little left to show
Of righted wrong and villainy requited!
Nay, Judgment now beginning upon earth,
Myself, methinks, in sight of all my wrongs,
Appointed heaven's avenging minister,
Accuser, judge, and executioner
Sword in hand, cite the guilty — First, as worst,
The usurper of his son's inheritance;
Him and his old accomplice, time and crime
Inveterate, and unable to repay
The golden years of life they stole away.
What, does he yet maintain his state, and keep
The throne he should be judged from? Down with him,
That I may trample on the false white head
So long has worn my crown! Where are my soldiers?
Of all my subjects and my vassals here
Not one to do my bidding? Hark! A trumpet!
The trumpet —

(He pauses as the trumpet sounds as in Act I.,
and masked Soldiers gradually fill in behind the Throne.)

KING (rising before his throne). Ay, indeed, the trumpet blows
A memorable note, to summon those
Who, if forthwith you fall not at the feet
Of him whose head you threaten with the dust,
Forthwith shall draw the curtain of the Past
About you; and this momentary gleam
Of glory that you think to hold life-fast,
So coming, so shall vanish, as a dream.

SEG. He prophesies; the old man prophesies;
And, at his trumpet's summons, from the tower

The leash-bound shadows loosen'd after me
  My rising glory reach and over-lour —
  But, reach not I my height, he shall not hold,
  But with me back to his own darkness!

(He dashes toward the throne and is enclosed by the soldiers.)

Traitors!
  Hold off! Unhand me! — Am not I your king?
  And you would strangle him! —
  But I am breaking with an inward Fire
  Shall scorch you off, and wrap me on the wings
  Of conflagration from a kindled pyre
  Of lying prophecies and prophet-kings
  Above the extinguish'd stars — Reach me the sword
  He flung me — Fill me such a bowl of wine
  As that you woke the day with —

KING. And shall close, —
  But of the vintage that Clotaldo knows.

(Exeunt.)

## ACT THE THIRD

### SCENE I

The Tower, etc., as in Act I. Scene I.

Segismund, as at first, and Clotaldo.

CLOTALDO.
  Princes and princesses, and counsellors
  Fluster'd to right and left — my life made at —
  But that was nothing
  Even the white-hair'd, venerable King

Seized on — Indeed, you made wild work of it;
And so discover'd in your outward action,
Flinging your arms about you in your sleep,
Grinding your teeth — and, as I now remember,
Woke mouthing out judgment and execution,
On those about you.

SEG. Ay, I did indeed.

CLO. Ev'n now your eyes stare wild; your hair stands up —
Your pulses throb and flutter, reeling still
Under the storm of such a dream —

SEG. A dream!
That seem'd as swearable reality
As what I wake in now.

CLO. Ay — wondrous how
Imagination in a sleeping brain
Out of the uncontingent senses draws
Sensations strong as from the real touch;
That we not only laugh aloud, and drench
With tears our pillow; but in the agony
Of some imaginary conflict, fight
And struggle — ev'n as you did; some, 'tis thought,
Under the dreamt-of stroke of death have died.

SEG. And what so very strange too — In that world
Where place as well as people all was strange,
Ev'n I almost as strange unto myself,
You only, you, Clotaldo — you, as much
And palpably yourself as now you are,
Came in this very garb you ever wore,
By such a token of the past, you said,
To assure me of that seeming present.

CLO. Ay?

SEG. Ay; and even told me of the very stars
  You tell me here of — how in spite of them,
  I was enlarged to all that glory.

CLO. Ay, By the false spirits' nice contrivance thus
  A little truth oft leavens all the false,
  The better to delude us.

SEG. For you know
  'Tis nothing but a dream?

CLO. Nay, you yourself
  Know best how lately you awoke from that
  You know you went to sleep on? —
  Why, have you never dreamt the like before?

SEG. Never, to such reality.

CLO. Such dreams
  Are oftentimes the sleeping exhalations
  Of that ambition that lies smouldering
  Under the ashes of the lowest fortune;
  By which, when reason slumbers, or has lost
  The reins of sensible comparison,
  We fly at something higher than we are —
  Scarce ever dive to lower — to be kings,
  Or conquerors, crown'd with laurel or with gold,
  Nay, mounting heaven itself on eagle wings.
  Which, by the way, now that I think of it,
  May furnish us the key to this high flight
  That royal Eagle we were watching, and
  Talking of as you went to sleep last night.

SEG. Last night? Last night?

CLO. Ay, do you not remember
Envying his immunity of flight,
As, rising from his throne of rock, he sail'd
Above the mountains far into the West,
That burn'd about him, while with poising wings
He darkled in it as a burning brand
Is seen to smoulder in the fire it feeds?

SEG. Last night — last night — Oh, what a day was that
Between that last night and this sad To-day!

CLO. And yet, perhaps,
Only some few dark moments, into which
Imagination, once lit up within
And unconditional of time and space,
Can pour infinities.

SEG. And I remember
How the old man they call'd the King, who wore
The crown of gold about his silver hair,
And a mysterious girdle round his waist,
Just when my rage was roaring at its height,
And after which it all was dark again,
Bid me beware lest all should be a dream.

CLO. Ay — there another specialty of dreams,
That once the dreamer 'gins to dream he dreams,
His foot is on the very verge of waking.

SEG. Would it had been upon the verge of death
That knows no waking —
Lifting me up to glory, to fall back,
Stunn'd, crippled — wretcheder than ev'n before.

CLO. Yet not so glorious, Segismund, if you

Your visionary honour wore so ill
As to work murder and revenge on those
Who meant you well.

SEG. Who meant me! — me! their Prince
Chain'd like a felon —

CLO. Stay, stay — Not so fast,
You dream'd the Prince, remember.

SEG. Then in dream
Revenged it only.

CLO. True. But as they say
Dreams are rough copies of the waking soul
Yet uncorrected of the higher Will,
So that men sometimes in their dreams confess
An unsuspected, or forgotten, self;
One must beware to check — ay, if one may,
Stifle ere born, such passion in ourselves
As makes, we see, such havoc with our sleep,
And ill reacts upon the waking day.
And, by the bye, for one test, Segismund,
Between such swearable realities —
Since Dreaming, Madness, Passion, are akin
In missing each that salutary rein
Of reason, and the guiding will of man:
One test, I think, of waking sanity
Shall be that conscious power of self-control,
To curb all passion, but much most of all
That evil and vindictive, that ill squares
With human, and with holy canon less,
Which bids us pardon ev'n our enemies,
And much more those who, out of no ill will,
Mistakenly have taken up the rod
Which heaven, they think, has put into their hands.

SEG. I think I soon shall have to try again —
Sleep has not yet done with me.

CLO. Such a sleep.
Take my advice — 'tis early yet — the sun
Scarce up above the mountain; go within,
And if the night deceived you, try anew
With morning; morning dreams they say come true.

SEG. Oh, rather pray for me a sleep so fast
As shall obliterate dream and waking too.

(Exit into the tower.)

CLO. So sleep; sleep fast: and sleep away those two
Night-potions, and the waking dream between
Which dream thou must believe; and, if to see
Again, poor Segismund! that dream must be. —
And yet, and yet, in these our ghostly lives,
Half night, half day, half sleeping, half awake,
How if our waking life, like that of sleep,
Be all a dream in that eternal life
To which we wake not till we sleep in death?
How if, I say, the senses we now trust
For date of sensible comparison, —
Ay, ev'n the Reason's self that dates with them,
Should be in essence or intensity
Hereafter so transcended, and awake
To a perceptive subtlety so keen
As to confess themselves befool'd before,
In all that now they will avouch for most?
One man — like this — but only so much longer
As life is longer than a summer's day,
Believed himself a king upon his throne,
And play'd at hazard with his fellows' lives,

Who cheaply dream'd away their lives to him.
The sailor dream'd of tossing on the flood:
The soldier of his laurels grown in blood:
The lover of the beauty that he knew
Must yet dissolve to dusty residue:
The merchant and the miser of his bags
Of finger'd gold; the beggar of his rags:
And all this stage of earth on which we seem
Such busy actors, and the parts we play'd,
Substantial as the shadow of a shade,
And Dreaming but a dream within a dream!

FIFE. Was it not said, sir,
By some philosopher as yet unborn,
That any chimney-sweep who for twelve hours
Dreams himself king is happy as the king
Who dreams himself twelve hours a chimney-sweep?

CLO. A theme indeed for wiser heads than yours
To moralize upon — How came you here? —

FIFE. Not of my own will, I assure you, sir.
No matter for myself: but I would know
About my mistress — I mean, master —

CLO. Oh, Now I remember — Well, your master-mistress
Is well, and deftly on its errand speeds,
As you shall — if you can but hold your tongue.
Can you?

FIFE. I'd rather be at home again.

CLO. Where you shall be the quicker if while here
You can keep silence.

FIFE. I may whistle, then?

Which by the virtue of my name I do,
And also as a reasonable test
Of waking sanity —

CLO. Well, whistle then;
And for another reason you forgot,
That while you whistle, you can chatter not.
Only remember — if you quit this pass —

FIFE. (His rhymes are out, or he had call'd it spot) —

CLO. A bullet brings you to.
I must forthwith to court to tell the King
The issue of this lamentable day,
That buries all his hope in night.
(To FIFE.)
Farewell. Remember.

FIFE. But a moment — but a word!
When shall I see my mis — mas —

CLO. Be content:
All in good time; and then, and not before,
Never to miss your master any more.
(Exit.)

FIFE. Such talk of dreaming — dreaming — I begin
To doubt if I be dreaming I am Fife,
Who with a lad who call'd herself a boy
Because — I doubt there's some confusion here —
He wore no petticoat, came on a time
Riding from Muscovy on half a horse,
Who must have dreamt she was a horse entire,
To cant me off upon my hinder face
Under this tower, wall-eyed and musket-tongued,
With sentinels a-pacing up and down,

Crying All's well when all is far from well,
All the day long, and all the night, until
I dream — if what is dreaming be not waking —
Of bells a-tolling and processions rolling
With candles, crosses, banners, San-benitos,
Of which I wear the flamy-finingest,
Through streets and places throng'd with fiery faces
To some back platform —
Oh, I shall take a fire into my hand
With thinking of my own dear Muscovy —
Only just over that Sierra there,
By which we tumbled headlong into — No-land.
Now, if without a bullet after me,
I could but get a peep of my old home
Perhaps of my own mule to take me there —
All's still — perhaps the gentlemen within
Are dreaming it is night behind their masks —
God send 'em a good nightmare! — Now then — Hark!
Voices — and up the rocks — and armed men
Climbing like cats — Puss in the corner then.

(He hides.)

(Enter Soldiers cautiously up the rocks.)

CAPTAIN.
 This is the frontier pass, at any rate,
 Where Poland ends and Muscovy begins.

SOLDIER.
 We must be close upon the tower, I know,
 That half way up the mountain lies ensconced.

CAPT. How know you that?

SOL. He told me so — the Page

Who put us on the scent.

SOL. 2. And, as I think,
 Will soon be here to run it down with us.

CAPT. Meantime, our horses on these ugly rocks
 Useless, and worse than useless with their clatter —
 Leave them behind, with one or two in charge,
 And softly, softly, softly.

SOLDIERS.
 — There it is!
 — There what?
 — The tower — the fortress —
 — That the tower! —
 — That mouse-trap! We could pitch it down the rocks
 With our own hands.
 — The rocks it hangs among
 Dwarf its proportions and conceal its strength;
 Larger and stronger than you think.
 — No matter;
 No place for Poland's Prince to be shut up in.
 At it at once!

CAPT. No — no — I tell you wait —
 Till those within give signal. For as yet
 We know not who side with us, and the fort
 Is strong in man and musket.

SOL. Shame to wait
 For odds with such a cause at stake.

CAPT. Because
 Of such a cause at stake we wait for odds —
 For if not won at once, for ever lost:
 For any long resistance on their part

Would bring Basilio's force to succour them
Ere we had rescued him we come to rescue.
So softly, softly, softly, still —

A SOLDIER (discovering Fife). Hilloa!

SOLDIERS.
— Hilloa! Here's some one skulking —
— Seize and gag him!
— Stab him at once, say I: the only way
To make all sure.
— Hold, every man of you!
And down upon your knees! — Why, 'tis the Prince!
— The Prince! —
— Oh, I should know him anywhere,
And anyhow disguised.
— But the Prince is chain'd.
— And of a loftier presence —
— 'Tis he, I tell you;
Only bewilder'd as he was before.
God save your Royal Highness! On our knees
Beseech you answer us!

FIFE. Just as you please.
Well — 'tis this country's custom, I suppose,
To take a poor man every now and then
And set him ON the throne; just for the fun
Of tumbling him again into the dirt.
And now my turn is come. 'Tis very pretty.

SOL. His wits have been distemper'd with their drugs.
But do you ask him, Captain.

CAPT. On my knees,
And in the name of all who kneel with me,
I do beseech your Highness answer to

Your royal title.

FIFE. Still, just as you please.
In my own poor opinion of myself —
But that may all be dreaming, which it seems
Is very much the fashion in this country
No Polish prince at all, but a poor lad
From Muscovy; where only help me back,
I promise never to contest the crown
Of Poland with whatever gentleman
You fancy to set up.

SOLDIERS.
— From Muscovy?
— A spy then —
— Of Astolfo's —
— Spy! a spy
— Hang him at once!

FIFE. No, pray don't dream of that!

SOL. How dared you then set yourself up for our Prince Segismund?

FIFE. *I* set up! — *I* like that
When 'twas yourselves be-siegesmunded me.

CAPT. No matter — Look! — The signal from the tower.
Prince Segismund!

SOL. (from the tower). Prince Segismund!

CAPT. All's well. Clotaldo safe secured? —

SOL. (from the tower). No — by ill luck,
Instead of coming in, as we had look'd for,

He sprang on horse at once, and off at gallop.

CAPT. To Court, no doubt — a blunder that — And yet
Perchance a blunder that may work as well
As better forethought. Having no suspicion
So will he carry none where his not going
Were of itself suspicious. But of those
Within, who side with us?

SOL. Oh, one and all
To the last man, persuaded or compell'd.

CAPT. Enough: whatever be to be retrieved
No moment to be lost. For though Clotaldo
Have no revolt to tell of in the tower,
The capital will soon awake to ours,
And the King's force come blazing after us.
Where is the Prince?

SOL. Within; so fast asleep
We woke him not ev'n striking off the chain
We had so cursedly help bind him with,
Not knowing what we did; but too ashamed
Not to undo ourselves what we had done.

CAPT. No matter, nor by whosesoever hands,
Provided done. Come; we will bring him forth
Out of that stony darkness here abroad,
Where air and sunshine sooner shall disperse
The sleepy fume which they have drugg'd him with.

(They enter the tower, and thence bring out Segismund asleep on a pallet, and set him in the middle of the stage.)

CAPT. Still, still so dead asleep, the very noise
And motion that we make in carrying him

Stirs not a leaf in all the living tree.

SOLDIERS.
 If living — But if by some inward blow
 For ever and irrevocably fell'd
 By what strikes deeper to the root than sleep?
 — He's dead! He's dead! They've kill'd him —
 — No — he breathes —
 And the heart beats — and now he breathes again
 Deeply, as one about to shake away
 The load of sleep.

CAPT. Come, let us all kneel round,
 And with a blast of warlike instruments,
 And acclamation of all loyal hearts,
 Rouse and restore him to his royal right,
 From which no royal wrong shall drive him more.

(They all kneel round his bed: trumpets, drums, etc.)

SOLDIERS.
 — Segismund! Segismund! Prince Segismund!
 — King Segismund! Down with Basilio!
 — Down with Astolfo! Segismund our King! etc.
 — He stares upon us wildly. He cannot speak.
 — I said so — driv'n him mad.
 — Speak to him, Captain.

CAPTAIN.
 Oh Royal Segismund, our Prince and King,
 Look on us — listen to us — answer us,
 Your faithful soldiery and subjects, now
 About you kneeling, but on fire to rise
 And cleave a passage through your enemies,
 Until we seat you on your lawful throne.
 For though your father, King Basilio,

Now King of Poland, jealous of the stars
That prophesy his setting with your rise,
Here holds you ignominiously eclipsed,
And would Astolfo, Duke of Muscovy,
Mount to the throne of Poland after him;
So will not we, your loyal soldiery
And subjects; neither those of us now first
Apprised of your existence and your right:
Nor those that hitherto deluded by
Allegiance false, their vizors now fling down,
And craving pardon on their knees with us
For that unconscious disloyalty,
Offer with us the service of their blood;
Not only we and they; but at our heels
The heart, if not the bulk, of Poland follows
To join their voices and their arms with ours,
In vindicating with our lives our own
Prince Segismund to Poland and her throne.

SOLDIERS.
— Segismund, Segismund, Prince Segismund!
— Our own King Segismund, etc.
(They all rise.)

SEG. Again? So soon? — What, not yet done with me?
The sun is little higher up, I think,
Than when I last lay down,
To bury in the depth of your own sea
You that infest its shallows.

CAPT. Sir!

SEG. And now,
Not in a palace, not in the fine clothes
We all were in; but here, in the old place,
And in our old accoutrement —

Only your vizors off, and lips unlock'd
To mock me with that idle title —

CAPT. Nay,
Indeed no idle title, but your own,
Then, now, and now for ever. For, behold,
Ev'n as I speak, the mountain passes fill
And bristle with the advancing soldiery
That glitters in your rising glory, sir;
And, at our signal, echo to our cry,
'Segismund, King of Poland!' etc.

(Shouts, trumpets, etc.)

SEG. Oh, how cheap
The muster of a countless host of shadows,
As impotent to do with as to keep!
All this they said before — to softer music.

CAPT. Soft music, sir, to what indeed were shadows,
That, following the sunshine of a Court,
Shall back be brought with it — if shadows still,
Yet to substantial reckoning.

SEG. They shall?
The white-hair'd and white-wanded chamberlain,
So busy with his wand too — the old King
That I was somewhat hard on — he had been
Hard upon me — and the fine feather'd Prince
Who crow'd so loud — my cousin, — and another,
Another cousin, we will not bear hard on —
And — But Clotaldo?

CAPT. Fled, my lord, but close
Pursued; and then —

SEG. Then, as he fled before,
  And after he had sworn it on his knees,
  Came back to take me — where I am! — No more,
  No more of this! Away with you! Begone!
  Whether but visions of ambitious night
  That morning ought to scatter, or grown out
  Of night's proportions you invade the day
  To scare me from my little wits yet left,
  Begone! I know I must be near awake,
  Knowing I dream; or, if not at my voice,
  Then vanish at the clapping of my hands,
  Or take this foolish fellow for your sport:
  Dressing me up in visionary glories,
  Which the first air of waking consciousness
  Scatters as fast as from the almander —
  That, waking one fine morning in full flower,
  One rougher insurrection of the breeze
  Of all her sudden honour disadorns
  To the last blossom, and she stands again
  The winter-naked scare-crow that she was!

CAPT. I know not what to do, nor what to say,
  With all this dreaming; I begin to doubt
  They have driv'n him mad indeed, and he and we
  Are lost together.

A SOLDIER (to Captain). Stay, stay; I remember —
  Hark in your ear a moment.
  (Whispers.)

CAPT. So — so — so? —
  Oh, now indeed I do not wonder, sir,
  Your senses dazzle under practices
  Which treason, shrinking from its own device,
  Would now persuade you only was a dream;
  But waking was as absolute as this

You wake in now, as some who saw you then,
Prince as you were and are, can testify:
Not only saw, but under false allegiance
Laid hands upon —

SOLDIER 1.
I, to my shame!

SOLDIER 2.
And I!

CAPT. Who, to wipe out that shame, have been the first
To stir and lead us — Hark!
(Shouts, trumpets, etc.)

A SOLDIER.
Our forces, sir,
Challenging King Basilio's, now in sight,
And bearing down upon us.

CAPT. Sir, you hear;
A little hesitation and delay,
And all is lost — your own right, and the lives
Of those who now maintain it at that cost;
With you all saved and won; without, all lost.
That former recognition of your right
Grant but a dream, if you will have it so;
Great things forecast themselves by shadows great:
Or will you have it, this like that dream too,
People, and place, and time itself, all dream
Yet, being in't, and as the shadows come
Quicker and thicker than you can escape,
Adopt your visionary soldiery,
Who, having struck a solid chain away,
Now put an airy sword into your hand,
And harnessing you piece-meal till you stand

Amidst us all complete in glittering,
If unsubstantial, steel —

ROSAURA (without). The Prince! The Prince!

CAPT. Who calls for him?

SOL. The Page who spurr'd us hither,
And now, dismounted from a foaming horse —

(Enter Rosaura)

ROSAURA.
Where is — but where I need no further ask
Where the majestic presence, all in arms,
Mutely proclaims and vindicates himself.

FIFE. My darling Lady-lord —

ROS. My own good Fife,
Keep to my side — and silence! — Oh, my Lord,
For the third time behold me here where first
You saw me, by a happy misadventure
Losing my own way here to find it out
For you to follow with these loyal men,
Adding the moment of my little cause
To yours; which, so much mightier as it is,
By a strange chance runs hand in hand with mine;
The self-same foe who now pretends your right,
Withholding mine — that, of itself alone,
I know the royal blood that runs in you
Would vindicate, regardless of your own:
The right of injured innocence; and, more,
Spite of this epicene attire, a woman's;
And of a noble stock I will not name
Till I, who brought it, have retrieved the shame.

Whom Duke Astolfo, Prince of Muscovy,
With all the solemn vows of wedlock won,
And would have wedded, as I do believe,
Had not the cry of Poland for a Prince
Call'd him from Muscovy to join the prize
Of Poland with the fair Estrella's eyes.
I, following him hither, as you saw,
Was cast upon these rocks; arrested by
Clotaldo: who, for an old debt of love
He owes my family, with all his might
Served, and had served me further, till my cause
Clash'd with his duty to his sovereign,
Which, as became a loyal subject, sir,
(And never sovereign had a loyaller,)
Was still his first. He carried me to Court,
Where, for the second time, I crossed your path;
Where, as I watch'd my opportunity,
Suddenly broke this public passion out;
Which, drowning private into public wrong,
Yet swiftlier sweeps it to revenge along.

SEG. Oh God, if this be dreaming, charge it not
To burst the channel of enclosing sleep
And drown the waking reason! Not to dream
Only what dreamt shall once or twice again
Return to buzz about the sleeping brain
Till shaken off for ever —
But reassailing one so quick, so thick —
The very figure and the circumstance
Of sense-confess'd reality foregone
In so-call'd dream so palpably repeated,
The copy so like the original,
We know not which is which; and dream so-call'd
Itself inweaving so inextricably
Into the tissue of acknowledged truth;
The very figures that empeople it

Returning to assert themselves no phantoms
In something so much like meridian day,
And in the very place that not my worst
And veriest disenchanter shall deny
For the too well-remember'd theatre
Of my long tragedy — Strike up the drums!
If this be Truth, and all of us awake,
Indeed a famous quarrel is at stake:
If but a Vision I will see it out,
And, drive the Dream, I can but join the rout.

CAPT. And in good time, sir, for a palpable
   Touchstone of truth and rightful vengeance too,
   Here is Clotaldo taken.

SOLDIERS.
   In with him!
   In with the traitor!

(Clotaldo brought in.)

SEG. Ay, Clotaldo, indeed —
   Himself — in his old habit — his old self —
   What! back again, Clotaldo, for a while
   To swear me this for truth, and afterwards
   All for a dreaming lie?

CLO. Awake or dreaming,
   Down with that sword, and down these traitors theirs,
   Drawn in rebellion 'gainst their Sovereign.

SEG. (about to strike). Traitor! Traitor yourself! —
   But soft — soft — soft! —
   You told me, not so very long ago,
   Awake or dreaming — I forget — my brain
   Is not so clear about it — but I know

One test you gave me to discern between,
Which mad and dreaming people cannot master;
Or if the dreamer could, so best secure
A comfortable waking — Was't not so?
(To Rosaura).
Needs not your intercession now, you see,
As in the dream before —
Clotaldo, rough old nurse and tutor too
That only traitor wert, to me if true —
Give him his sword; set him on a fresh horse;
Conduct him safely through my rebel force;
And so God speed him to his sovereign's side!
Give me your hand; and whether all awake
Or all a-dreaming, ride, Clotaldo, ride —
Dream-swift — for fear we dreams should overtake.

(A Battle may be supposed to take place; after which)

## ACT THE FOURTH

## SCENE I

A wooded pass near the field of battle:

drums, trumpets, firing, etc. Cries of 'God save Basilio! Segismund,' etc.

(Enter Fife, running.)

FIFE. God save them both, and save them all! say I! —
Oh — what hot work! — Whichever way one turns
The whistling bullet at one's ears — I've drifted
Far from my mad young — master — whom I saw
Tossing upon the very crest of battle,
Beside the Prince — God save her first of all!
With all my heart I say and pray — and so
Commend her to His keeping — bang! — bang! — bang!
And for myself — scarce worth His thinking of —
I'll see what I can do to save myself
Behind this rock, until the storm blows over.

(Skirmishes, shouts, firing, etc. After some time enter King Basilio, Astolfo, and Clotaldo)

KING. The day is lost!

AST. Do not despair — the rebels —

KING. Alas! the vanquish'd only are the rebels.

CLOTALDO. Ev'n if this battle lost us, 'tis but one
Gain'd on their side, if you not lost in it;
Another moment and too late: at once
Take horse, and to the capital, my liege,

Where in some safe and holy sanctuary
  Save Poland in your person.

AST. Be persuaded:
  You know your son: have tasted of his temper;
  At his first onset threatening unprovoked
  The crime predicted for his last and worst.
  How whetted now with such a taste of blood,
  And thus far conquest!

KING. Ay, and how he fought!
  Oh how he fought, Astolfo; ranks of men
  Falling as swathes of grass before the mower;
  I could but pause to gaze at him, although,
  Like the pale horseman of the Apocalypse,
  Each moment brought him nearer — Yet I say,
  I could but pause and gaze on him, and pray
  Poland had such a warrior for her king.

AST. The cry of triumph on the other side
  Gains ground upon us here — there's but a moment
  For you, my liege, to do, for me to speak,
  Who back must to the field, and what man may
  Do, to retrieve the fortune of the day.
  (Firing.)

FIFE (falling forward, shot). Oh, Lord, have mercy on me.

KING. What a shriek —
  Oh, some poor creature wounded in a cause
  Perhaps not worth the loss of one poor life! —
  So young too — and no soldier —

FIFE. A poor lad,
  Who choosing play at hide and seek with death,
  Just hid where death just came to look for him;

For there's no place, I think, can keep him out,
Once he's his eye upon you. All grows dark —
You glitter finely too — Well — we are dreaming
But when the bullet's off — Heaven save the mark!
So tell my mister — mastress —
(Dies.)

KING. Oh God! How this poor creature's ignorance
Confounds our so-call'd wisdom! Even now
When death has stopt his lips, the wound through which
His soul went out, still with its bloody tongue
Preaching how vain our struggle against fate!

(Voices within).
After them! After them! This way! This way!
The day is ours — Down with Basilio, etc.

AST. Fly, sir —

KING. And slave-like flying not out-ride
The fate which better like a King abide!

(Enter Segismund, Rosaura, Soldiers, etc.)

SEG. Where is the King?

KING (prostrating himself). Behold him, — by this late
Anticipation of resistless fate,
Thus underneath your feet his golden crown,
And the white head that wears it, laying down,
His fond resistance hope to expiate.

SEG. Princes and warriors of Poland — you
That stare on this unnatural sight aghast,
Listen to one who, Heaven-inspired to do
What in its secret wisdom Heaven forecast,

By that same Heaven instructed prophet-wise
To justify the present in the past.
What in the sapphire volume of the skies
Is writ by God's own finger misleads none,
But him whose vain and misinstructed eyes,
They mock with misinterpretation,
Or who, mistaking what he rightly read,
Ill commentary makes, or misapplies
Thinking to shirk or thwart it. Which has done
The wisdom of this venerable head;
Who, well provided with the secret key
To that gold alphabet, himself made me,
Himself, I say, the savage he fore-read
Fate somehow should be charged with; nipp'd the growth
Of better nature in constraint and sloth,
That only bring to bear the seed of wrong
And turn'd the stream to fury whose out-burst
Had kept his lawful channel uncoerced,
And fertilized the land he flow'd along.
Then like to some unskilful duellist,
Who having over-reached himself pushing too hard
His foe, or but a moment off his guard —
What odds, when Fate is one's antagonist! —
Nay, more, this royal father, self-dismay'd
At having Fate against himself array'd,
Upon himself the very sword he knew
Should wound him, down upon his bosom drew,
That might well handled, well have wrought; or, kept
Undrawn, have harmless in the scabbard slept.
But Fate shall not by human force be broke,
Nor foil'd by human feint; the Secret learn'd
Against the scholar by that master turn'd
Who to himself reserves the master-stroke.
Witness whereof this venerable Age,
Thrice crown'd as Sire, and Sovereign, and Sage,
Down to the very dust dishonour'd by

The very means he tempted to defy
The irresistible. And shall not I,
Till now the mere dumb instrument that wrought
The battle Fate has with my father fought,
Now the mere mouth-piece of its victory
Oh, shall not I, the champions' sword laid down,
Be yet more shamed to wear the teacher's gown,
And, blushing at the part I had to play,
Down where that honour'd head I was to lay
By this more just submission of my own,
The treason Fate has forced on me atone?

KING. Oh, Segismund, in whom I see indeed,
Out of the ashes of my self-extinction
A better self revive; if not beneath
Your feet, beneath your better wisdom bow'd,
The Sovereignty of Poland I resign,
With this its golden symbol; which if thus
Saved with its silver head inviolate,
Shall nevermore be subject to decline;
But when the head that it alights on now
Falls honour'd by the very foe that must,
As all things mortal, lay it in the dust,
Shall star-like shift to his successor's brow.

(Shouts, trumpets, etc. God save King Segismund!)

SEG. For what remains —
As for my own, so for my people's peace,
Astolfo's and Estrella's plighted hands
I disunite, and taking hers to mine,
His to one yet more dearly his resign.

(Shouts, etc. God save Estrella, Queen of Poland!)

SEG (to Clotaldo). You

That with unflinching duty to your King,
Till countermanded by the mightier Power,
Have held your Prince a captive in the tower,
Henceforth as strictly guard him on the throne
No less my people's keeper than my own.
You stare upon me all, amazed to hear
The word of civil justice from such lips
As never yet seem'd tuned to such discourse.
But listen — In that same enchanted tower,
Not long ago I learn'd it from a dream
Expounded by this ancient prophet here;
And which he told me, should it come again,
How I should bear myself beneath it; not
As then with angry passion all on fire,
Arguing and making a distemper'd soul;
But ev'n with justice, mercy, self-control,
As if the dream I walk'd in were no dream,
And conscience one day to account for it.
A dream it was in which I thought myself,
And you that hail'd me now then hail'd me King,
In a brave palace that was all my own,
Within, and all without it, mine; until,
Drunk with excess of majesty and pride,
Methought I tower'd so high and swell'd so wide,
That of myself I burst the glittering bubble,
That my ambition had about me blown,
And all again was darkness. Such a dream
As this in which I may be walking now;
Dispensing solemn justice to you shadows,
Who make believe to listen; but anon,
With all your glittering arms and equipage,
King, princes, captains, warriors, plume and steel,
Ay, ev'n with all your airy theatre,
May flit into the air you seem to rend
With acclamation, leaving me to wake
In the dark tower; or dreaming that I wake

From this that waking is; or this and that
Both waking or both dreaming; such a doubt
Confounds and clouds our mortal life about.
And, whether wake or dreaming, this I know,
How dream-wise human glories come and go;
Whose momentary tenure not to break,
Walking as one who knows he soon may wake,
So fairly carry the full cup, so well
Disorder'd insolence and passion quell,
That there be nothing after to upbraid
Dreamer or doer in the part he play'd,
Whether To-morrow's dawn shall break the spell,
Or the Last Trumpet of the eternal Day,
When Dreaming with the Night shall pass away.
(Exeunt.)

# THE PURGATORY OF ST. PATRICK

## Translated by Denis Florence MacCarthy

### PERSONS

EGERIUS, King of Ireland.
PATRICK.
LUIS ENIUS.
A GOOD ANGEL.
A BAD ANGEL.
PHILIP.
LEOGAIRE.
A CAPTAIN.
POLONIA, Daughter of the King.
LESBIA, her Sister.
PAUL, a Peasant.
LUCY, his Wife.
Two Canons Regular.
Two Peasants.
An Old Countryman.
A Muffled Figure.
Attendants, Friars, and others.

The Scene passes in Ireland, in the Court of King Egerius, and other parts.

### ACT THE FIRST.

THE SEA-SHORE, WITH PRECIPITOUS CLIFFS.

### SCENE I.

The King EGERIUS, clad in skins, LEOGAIRE, POLONIA, LESBIA, and a Captain.

KING (furious). Here let me die. Away!

LEOGAIRE. Oh, stop, my lord!

CAPTAIN. Consider . . .

LESBIA. Listen . . .

POLONIA. Stay . . .

KING. Yes, from this rocky height,
Nigh to the sun, that with one starry light
Its rugged brow doth crown,
Headlong among the salt waves leaping down
Let him descend who so much pain perceives;
There let him raging die who raging lives.

LESBIA. Why wildly seekest thou the sea?

POLONIA. Thou wert asleep, my lord; what could it be?

KING. Every torment that doth dwell
For ever with the thirsty fiends of hell —
Dark brood of that dread mother,
The seven-necked snake, whose poisoned breath doth smother
The fourth celestial sphere;
In fine, its horror and its misery drear
Within me reach so far,
That I myself upon myself make war,
When in the arms of sleep
A living corse am I, for it doth keep
Such mastery o'er my life, that, as I dream,
A pale foreshadowing threat of coming death I seem.

POLONIA. How could a dream, my lord, provoke you so?

KING. Alas! my daughters, listen, you shall know.
From out the lips of a most lovely youth
(And though a miserable slave, in sooth
I dare not hurt him, and I speak his praise),
Well, from the mouth of a poor slave, a blaze
Of lambent lustre came,
Which mildly burned in rays of gentlest flame;
Till reaching you,
The living fire at once consumed ye two.
I stood betwixt ye both, and though I sought
To stay its fury, the strange fire would not
Molest or wound me, passing like the wind,
So that despairing, blind,
I woke from out a deep abysm
Of dream, a lethargy, a paroxysm;
But find my pains the same,
For still it seems to me I see that flame,
And flying, at every turn
See you consumed; but now I also burn.

LESBIA. Light phantoms these,
Chimeras which an entrance find with ease
Into the dreamer's brain.
(A trumpet sounds.
But wherefore sounds this trumpet?

CAPTAIN. It is plain
Ships are approaching to our port below.

POLONIA. Grant me thy leave, great lord, since thou dost know
A trumpet in my ear
Sounds like a siren's voice, serene and clear;
Ever to war inclined,
In martial music my chief joy I find;
Its clangour and its din
Lead my rapt senses on: for I may win

Through it my highest fame,
When soaring to the sun on waves of flame,
Or wings as swift, my proud name shall ascend,
There it may be with Pallas to contend.
(Aside.
A stronger motive urges me to go:
If it is Philip's ship I wish to know.
(Exit.

LEOGAIRE. Descend, my lord, with me
Down where the foam-curled head of the blue sea
Bows at the base of this majestic hill,
Whose sands, like chains of gold, restrain its wilder will.

CAPTAIN. Let it divert thy care,
This snow-white monster fair,
Whose waves of dazzling hue
Shape silver frames round mirrors sapphire blue.

KING. Nothing can give relief;
Nothing can now divert me from my grief;
That mystic fire will give my life no rest, —
My heart an Etna seems within my breast.

LESBIA. Is any sight more fair? can aught surpass
That of a vessel breaking through the glass
Of crystal seas, and seeming there to be,
As with light share it cuts the azure mass,
A fish of the wind, a swift bird of the sea,
And being for two elements designed,
Flies in the wave and swims upon the wind?
But now no witchery
Were it to any eyes that sight to see;
For lo! the roused-up ocean,
Heaving with all its mountain waves in motion,
Wrinkles its haughty brow,

And suddenly awaking,
Neptune, his trident shaking,
Ruffles the beauteous face so sweet and calm but now.
Well may the sailor in his floating home
Expect a storm, for, lo! in heaven's high vault
Rise pyramids of ice, mountains of salt,
Turrets of snow, and palaces of foam.

POLONIA returns.

POLONIA. O dire misfortune!

KING. What so suddenly
Has chanced, Polonia?

POLONIA. This inconstant sea,
This Babel of wild waves that seeks heaven's gate,
So great its fury, and its rage so great,
Driven by a drought accursed,
(Who would have thought that waves themselves could thirst?)
Has swallowed in the depths of its dread womb,
But now, a numerous company, to whom
It consecrates below
Red sepulchres of coral, tombs of snow,
In silver-shining caves;
For from their prison out o'er all the waves
Has Aeolus the winds let loose, and they,
Without a law to guide them on their way,
Fell on that bark from which the trumpet rang,
A swan whose own sad obsequies it sang.
I from that cliff's stupendous height,
Which dares to intercept the great sun's light,
Looked full of hope along that vessel's track,
To see if it was Philip who came back;
Philip whose flag had borne upon the breeze
Thy royal arms triumphant through the seas;

When his sad wreck swept by,
And every sound was buried in a sigh,
His ruin seemed not wrought by seas or skies,
But by my lips and eyes,
Because my cries, the tears that made me blind,
Increased still more the water and the wind.

KING. How! ye immortal deities,
Would you still try by threatenings such as these
What I can bear?
Is it your wish that I should mount and tear
This azure palace down, as if the shape
Of a new Nimrod I assumed, to show
How on my shoulders might the world escape,
Nor as I gazed below
Feel any fear, though all the abysses under
Were rent with fire and flame, with lightning and with thunder.

### SCENE II.

PATRICK, and then LUIS ENIUS.

PATRICK (within). Ah me!

LEOGAIRE. Some mournful voice.

KING. What's this?

CAPTAIN. The form,
As of a man who has escaped the storm,
Swims yonder to the land.

LESBIA. And strives to give a life-sustaining hand
Unto another wretch, when he
Appeared about to sink in death's last agony.

POLONIA. Poor traveller from afar,
Whom evil fate and thy malignant star
On this far shore have cast,
Let my voice guide thee, if amid the blast
My accents thou canst hear; since it is only
To rouse thy courage that I speak to thee.
Come!

(Enter PATRICK and LUIS ENIUS, clasping each other.

PATRICK. Oh, God save me!

LUIS. Oh, the devil save ME!

LESBIA. They move my pity, these unhappy two.

KING. Not mine, for what it is I never knew.

PATRICK. Oh, sirs, if wretchedness
Can move most hearts to pity man's distress,
I will not think that here
A heart can be so cruel and severe
As to repel a wretch from out the wave.
Pity, for God's sake, at your feet I crave.

LUIS. I don't, for I disdain it.
From God or man I never hope to gain it.

KING. Say who you are; we then shall know
What hospitable care your needs we owe.
But first I will inform you of my name,
Lest ignorance of that perchance might claim
Exemption from respect, and words be said
Unworthy of the deference and the dread
That here my subjects show me,
Or wanting the due homage that you owe me.

I am the King Egerius,
The worthy lord of this small realm, for thus
I call it being mine;
Till 'tis the world, my sword shall not resign
Its valorous hope. The dress,
Not of a king, but of wild savageness
I wear: to testify,
Thus seeming a wild beast, how wild am I.
No god my worship claims;
I do not even know the deities' names:
Here they no service nor respect receive;
To die and to be born is all that we believe.
Now that you know how much you should revere
My royal state, say who you are.

PATRICK. Then hear:
Patrick is my name, my country
Ireland, and an humble hamlet,
Scarcely known to men, called Empthor,
Is my place of birth: It standeth
Midway 'twixt the north and west,
On a mountain which is guarded
As a prison by the sea, —
In the island which hereafter
Will be called the Isle of Saints,
To its glory everlasting;
Such a crowd, great lord, therein
Will give up their lives as martyrs
In religious attestation
Of the faith, faith's highest marvel.
Of an Irish cavalier,
And of his chaste spouse and partner,
A French lady, I was born,
Unto whom I owe (oh, happy
That 'twas so!), beyond my birthright
Of nobility, the vantage

Of the Christian faith, the light
Of Christ's true religion granted
In the sacred rite of baptism,
Which a mark indelibly stampeth
On the soul, heaven's gate, as it
Is the sacrament first granted
By the Church. My pious parents,
Having thus the debt exacted
From all married people paid
By my birth, retired thereafter
To two separate convents, where
In the purity and calmness
Of their chaste abodes they lived,
Till the fatal line of darkness,
Ending life, was reached, and they,
Fortified by every practice
Of the Catholic faith, in peace
Yielded up their souls in gladness,
Unto heaven their spirits giving,
Giving unto earth their ashes.
I, an orphan, then remained
Carefully and kindly guarded
By a very holy matron,
Underneath whose rule I hardly
Had completed one brief lustrum —
Five short years had scarce departed —
Five bright circles of the sun
Wheeling round on golden axles,
Twelve high zodiac signs illuming
And one earthly sphere, when happened
Through me an event that showed
God's omnipotence and marvels;
Since of weakest instruments
God makes use of, to enhance his
Majesty the more, to show
That for what men think the grandest

And most strange effects, to Him
Should alone the praise be granted. —
It so happened, and Heaven knoweth
That it is not pride, but rather
Pure religious zeal, that men
Should know how the Lord hath acted,
Makes me tell it, that one day
To my doors a blind man rambled,
Gormas was his name, who said,
"God who sends me here commands thee
In His name to give me sight;"
I, obedient to the mandate,
Made at once the sign of the cross
On his sightless eyes, that started
Into life and light once more
From their state of utter darkness.
At another time when heaven,
Muffled in the thickest, blackest
Clouds, made war upon the world,
Hurling at it lightning lances
Of white snow, which fell so thickly
On a mountain, that soon after
They being melted by the sun,
So filled up our streets and alleys,
So inundated our houses,
That amid the wild waves stranded
They were ships of bricks and stones,
Barks of cement and of plaster.
Who before saw waves on mountains?
Who 'mid woods saw ships at anchor?
I the sign of the cross then made
On the waters, and in accents,
In a tone of grave emotion,
In God's name the waves commanded
To retire: they turned that moment
And left dry the lands they ravaged.

Oh, great God! who will not praise Thee?
Who will not confess Thee Master? —
Other wonders I could tell you,
But my modesty throws shackles
On my tongue, makes mute my voice,
And my lips seals up and fastens.
I grew up, in fine, inclined
Less to arms than to the marvels
Knowledge can reveal: I gave me
Almost wholly up to master
Sacred Science, to the reading
Of the Lives of Saints, a practice
Which doth teach us faith, hope, zeal,
Charity and Christian manners.
In these studies thus immersed,
I one day approached the margin
Of the sea with some young friends,
Fellow-students and companions,
When a bark drew nigh, from which
Suddenly out-leaping landed
Armed men, fierce pirates they,
Who these seas, these islands, ravaged;
We at once were captives made,
And in order not to hazard
Losing us their prey, they sailed
Out to sea with swelling canvas.
Of this daring pirate boat
Philip de Roqui was the captain,
In whose breast, for his destruction,
Pride, the poisonous weed, was planted.
He the Irish seas and coast
Having thus for some days ravaged,
Taking property and life,
Pillaging our homes and hamlets;
But myself alone reserved
To be offered as a vassal,

As a slave to thee, O king!
In thy presence as he fancied.
Oh! how ignorant is man,
When of God's wise laws regardless,
When, without consulting Him,
He his future projects planneth!
Philip well, at sea might say so;
Since to-day, in sight of land here,
Heaven the while being all serene,
Mild the air, the water tranquil,
In an instant, in a moment,
He beheld his proud hopes blasted.
In the hollow-breasted waves
Roared the wind, the sea grew maddened,
Billows upon billows rolled
Mountain high, and wildly dashed them
Wet against the sun, as if
They its light would quench and darken.
The poop-lantern of our ship
Seemed a comet most erratic —
Seemed a moving exhalation,
Or a star from space outstarted;
At another time it touched
The profoundest deep sea-caverns,
Or the treacherous sands whereon
Ran the stately ship and parted.
Then the fatal waves became
Monuments of alabaster,
Tombs of coral and of pearl.
I (and why this boon was granted
Unto me by Heaven I know not,
Being so useless), with expanded
Arms, struck out, but not alone
My own life to save, nay rather
In the attempt to save this brave
Young man here, that life to barter;

For I know not by what secret
Instinct towards him I'm attracted;
And I think he yet will pay me
Back this debt with interest added.
Finally, through Heaven's great pity
We at length have happily landed,
Where my misery may expect it,
Or my better fate may grant it;
Since we are your slaves and servants,
That being moved by our disasters,
That being softened by our weeping,
Our sore plight may melt your hardness,
Our affliction force your kindness,
And our very pains command you.

KING. Silence, miserable Christian,
For my very soul seems fastened
On thy words, compelling me,
How I know not, to regard thee
With strange reverence and fear,
Thinking thou must be that vassal —
That poor slave whom in my dream
I beheld outbreathing flashes,
Saw outflashing living fire,
In whose flame, so lithe and lambent,
My Polonia and my Lesbia
Like poor moths were burned to ashes.

PATRICK. Know, the flame that from my mouth
Issued, is the true Evangel,
Is the doctrine of the Gospel: —
'Tis the word which I'm commanded
Unto thee to preach, O King!
To thy subjects and thy vassals,
To thy daughters, who shall be
Christians through its means.

KING. Cease, fasten
Thy presumptuous lips, vile Christian,
For thy words insult and stab me.

LESBIA. Stay!

POLONIA. And wilt thou in thy pity
Try to save him from his anger?

LESBIA. Yes.

POLONIA. Forbear, and let him die.

LESBIA. Thus to die by a king's hands here
Were unjust. (Aside.) (It is my pity
For these Christians prompts my answer.)

POLONIA. If this second Joseph then,
Like the first one, would unravel,
Would interpret the king's dreams,
Do not dread the result, my father;
For if my being seen to burn
Indicates in any manner
I should ever be a Christian,
As impossible a marvel
Such would be, as if, being dead,
I could rise and live thereafter.
But in order that your mind
May be turned from such just anger,
Let us hear now who this other
Stranger is.

LUIS. Then be attentive,
Beautiful divinity,
For my history thus commences: —

Great Egerius, King of Ireland,
I by name am Luis Enius,
And a Christian also, this
Being the sole point of resemblance
Betwixt Patrick and myself,
Yet a difference presenting:
For although we two are Christians,
So distinct and so dissevered
Are we, that not good from evil
Is more opposite in its essence.
Yet for all that, in defence
Of the faith I believe and reverence,
I would lose a thousand lives
(Such the esteem for it I cherish).
Yes, by God! The oath alone
Shows how firmly I confess Him.
I no pious tales or wonders,
Worked in my behalf by Heaven,
Have to speak of: no; dark crimes,
Robberies, murders, sacrileges,
Treasons, treacheries, betrayals,
Must I tell instead, however
Vain it be in me to glory
In my having such effected.
I in one of Ireland's many
Isles was born; the planets seven,
I suspect, in wild abnormal
Interchange of influences,
Must have at my hapless birth-time
All their various gifts presented.
Fickleness the Moon implanted
In my nature; subtle Hermes
With and genius ill-employed;
(Better ne'er to have possessed them);
Wanton Venus gave me passions —
All the flatteries of the senses,

And stern Mars a cruel mind
(Mars and Venus both together
What will they not give?); the Sun
Gave to me an easy temper,
Prone to spend, and when means failed me
Theft and robbery were my helpers;
Jupiter presumptuous pride,
Thoughts fantastic and unfettered,
Gave me; Saturn, rage and anger,
Valour and a will determined
On its ends; and from such causes
Followed the due consequences.
Here from Ireland being banished,
By a cause I do not mention
Through respect to him, my father
Came to Perpignan, and settled
In that Spanish town, when I
Scarce my first ten years had ended,
And when sixteen came, he died.
May God rest his soul in heaven! —
Orphaned, I remained the prey
Of my passions and my pleasures,
O'er whose tempting plain I ran
Without rein or curb to check me.
The two poles of my existence,
On which all the rest depended
For support, were play and women.
What a base on which to rest me!
Here my tongue would not be able
To acquaint you 'in extenso'
With my actions: a brief abstract
May, however, be attempted.
I, to outrage a young maiden,
Stabbed to death a noble elder,
Her own father: for the sake
Of his wife, a most respected

Cavalier I slew, as he
Lay beside her in the helpless
State of sleep, his honour bathing
In his blood, the bed presenting
A sad theatre of crimes,
Murder and adultery blended.
Thus the father and the husband
Life for honour's sake surrendered;
For even honour has its martyrs.
May God rest their souls in heaven! —
Dreading punishment for this,
I fled hastily, and entered
France, where my exploits, methinks,
Time will cease not to remember;
For, assisting in the wars
Which at that time were contended
Bravely betwixt France and England,
I took military service
Under Stephen, the French king,
And a fight which chance presented
Showed my courage to be such,
That the king himself, as guerdon
Of my valour, gave to me
The commission of an ensign.
How that debt I soon repaid,
I prefer not now to tell thee.
Back to Perpignan, thus honoured,
I returned, and having entered
Once a guard-house there to play,
For some trifle I lost temper,
Struck a serjeant, killed a captain,
And maimed others there assembled.
At the cries from every quarter
Speedily the watch collected,
And in flying to a church,
As they hurried to prevent me,

I a catch-pole killed. ('Twas something
One good work to have effected
'Mid so many that were bad.)
May God rest his soul in heaven! —
Far I fled into the country,
And asylum found and shelter
In a convent of religious,
Which was founded in that desert,
Where I lived retired and hidden,
Well taken care of and attended.
For a lady there, a nun,
Was my cousin, which connection
Gave to her the special burden
Of this care. My heart already
Being a basilisk which turned
All the honey into venom,
Passing swiftly from mere liking
To desire — that monster ever
Feeding on the impossible —
Living fire that with intensest
Fury burns when most opposed —
Flame the wind revives and strengthens,
False, deceitful, treacherous foe
Which doth murder its possessor —
In a word, desire in him,
Who nor God nor law respecteth,
Of the horrible, of the shocking,
Thinks but only to attempt it. —
Yes, I dared . . . . But here disturbed,
When, my lord, I this remember,
Mute the voice in horror fails,
Sad the accent faints and trembles,
And as 'mid the night's dark shadows,
The hair stands on end through terror;
Thus confused, so full of doubt,
Sad remembrance so o'erwhelms me,

That the thing I dared to do
I scarce dare in words to tell thee.
For, in fine, my crime is such,
So to be abhorred, detested,
So profane, so sacrilegious
(Strange upon thee so to press it),
That for having such committed
I at times feel some repentance.
Well, in fine, I dared one night,
When deep silence had erected
Sepulchres of fleeting sleep
For men's overwearied senses,
When a dark and cloudy veil
Heaven had o'er its face extended —
Mourning which the wind assumed
For the sun whose life had ended —
In whose obsequies the night-birds
Swan-notes sang instead of verses,
And when back from waves of sapphire,
Where their beauty was reflected,
The clear stars a second time
Trembling lights to heaven presented: —
Well, on such a night, by climbing
O'er the garden wall, I entered
With the assistance of two friends
(For when such things are attempted
An associate never fails),
And in horror and in terror,
Seeking in the dark my death,
Reached at length the cell (I tremble
To remember it) in which
Was my cousin, whom respectful
Silence bids me not to name,
Though all self-respect has left me.
Frightened at such nameless horror,
On the hard floor she fell senseless,

When she passed into my arms,
And ere she regained her senses,
She already was outside
Her asylum, in a desert,
When if heaven possessed the power,
It had not the will to help her.
Women, when they are persuaded
That the wildest of excesses
Are the effects of love, forgive them
Easily; and, therefore, pleasure
Following tears, some consolation
In her miseries was effected;
Though, in fact, they were so great,
That united in one person
She saw violence, violation,
Incest, nay, adultery even,
Against God who was her spouse,
And a sacrilege most dreadful.
Finally we left that place,
Being carried to Valencia
By two steeds that well might claim
From the winds to be descended:
Feigning that she was my wife,
But with little peace we dwelt there;
For I quickly having squandered
Whatsoever little treasure
I brought with me, without friends,
p 260
Without any hope of help there,
In my dire distress appealed
To the beauty still so perfect
Of my poor pretended wife:
If for aught I did I ever
Could feel shame, this act alone
Would most surely overwhelm me;
Since it is the lowest baseness

That the vilest breast descends to,
To put up to sale one's honour,
And to trade in love's caresses.
Scarce with shameless front had I
This base plan to her suggested,
When concealing her design
She gave seeming acquiescence;
But I scarce had turned my back,
Hardly had I left her presence,
When she, flying from me, found
Grace a convent's walls to enter.
There, a holy monk advising,
She a saving port and shelter
Found against the world's wild storms,
And there died, her sin, her penance,
Giving all a great example;
May God rest her soul in heaven! —
Seeing that the narrow world
Now took note of my offences,
And that soon the very land
Might reject me, I determined
To re-seek my native country;
For at least I there expected
To be safer from my foes,
In a place so long my centre
And my home. The way I took
And to Ireland came, which welcomed
Me at first as would a mother,
But a step-mother resembled
Before long, for seeking a passage
Where a harbour lay protected
By a mole, I found that corsairs
Lay concealed within the shelter
Of a little creek which his
Out of view their well-armed vessel.
And of these, their captain, Philip,

Took me prisoner, after efforts
Made in my defence so brave,
That in deference to the mettle
I displayed, my life he spared.
What ensured you know already,
How the wind in sudden anger
Rising into raging tempest,
Now chastised us in its pride,
Now our lives more cruelly threatened,
Making in the seas and mountains
Such wild ruin and resemblance,
That to mock the mountain's pride
Waves still mightier forms presented,
Which with catapults of crystal
Made the cliffs' foundations tremble,
So that neighbouring cities fell,
And the sea, in scornful temper,
Gathering up from its abysses
The munition it collecteth,
Fired upon the land its pearls
In their shells, wherein engendered
By the swift breath of the morning
In its dew, they shine resplendent
Tears of ice and fire; in fine,
Not in pictures so imperfect
All our time to waste, the crew
Went to sup in the infernal
Halls themselves; I, too, a guest
Would have equally attended
With them, if this Patrick, here,
Whom I know not why I reverence,
Looking with respect and fear
On his beauteous countenance ever,
Had not drawn me from the sea,
Where, exhausted, sinking, helpless,
I drank death in every draught,

Agony in each salt wave's venom.
This my history is, and now
I wish neither life nor mercy,
Neither that my pains should move thee,
Nor my asking should compel thee,
Save in this, to give me death,
That thus may the life be ended
Of a man who is so bad,
That he scarcely can be better.

KING. Luis, though thou art a Christian,
Which by me is most detested,
Yet I so admire thy courage
That I wish, before all present,
Between thee and him to show
How my power can be exerted,
How it punishes as rewards,
How it elevates and depresses.
And so thus my arms I give thee,
That within them thus extended
Thou may'st reach my heart; to thee
Thus beneath my feet to tread thee;
(He throws PATRICK on the ground and places his foot upon him.
The two actions signifying
How the heavier scale descendeth.
And that, Patrick, thou may'st see
How I value or give credit
To thy threats, thy life I spare.
Vomit forth the flame incessant
Of the so-called word of God,
That by this thou may'st be certain
I do not adore his Godship,
Nor his miracles have dread of.
Live then; but in such a state
Of poor, mean, and abject service,

As befits a useless hind
In the fields; and so as shepherd
I would have thee guard my flocks,
Which are in these vales collected.
Let us see, if for the purpose
Of this mystic fire outspreading,
Being my slave, thy God will free thee
From captivity and thy fetters.
(Exit.

LESBIA. Patrick moves my heart to pity.
(Exit.

POLONIA. Not so mine, for none I cherish.
Had I any, none would move me
Sooner than this Luis Enius.
(Exit.

## SCENE III.

PATRICK and LUIS.

PATRICK. Luis, though a low position
Mine is here, and I observe thee
Raised to fortune's highest summit,
Yet I feel more grief than envy
At thy rise. Thou art a Christian;
Show thyself one now in earnest.

LUIS. Patrick, let me now enjoy
The first favours fate has sent me
After so much sad misfortune.

PATRICK. One word, then (if thou wilt let me
So presume), I ask of thee.

LUIS. What is that?

PATRICK. Upon this earth here,
Once again, alive or dead,
That we two shall meet together.

LUIS. Such a word dost ask me?

PATRICK. Yes.

LUIS. Then I give it.

PATRICK. I accept it.
(Exeunt.

### SCENE IV.

A HAMLET NEAR THE COURT OF EGERIUS.

PHILIP and LUCY.

LUCY. Pardon, if I have not known
How to serve you as I ought.

PHILIP. For much more than you have thought
Must you my forgiveness own.
For when I your kind face view,
Pain and pleasure being at war,
I have much to thank you for,
And have much to pardon too.
Thanks, with which my heart is rife,
Are for life restored and breath;
Pardon, for you give me death,
As before you gave me life.

LUCY. For such flattering declarations

Rude and ignorant am I,
So my arms will give reply;
Which gets rid of explanations.
Let their silent interfacing
Figure what my words should be.

## SCENE V.

PAUL. — THE SAME.

PAUL (aside). Eh, sirs! what is this I see?
Some one here my wife's embracing.
What's to do? I burn, I burst.
Kill her? Yes. 'Twas fortune sent me.
One thing only doth prevent me,
Which is, she might kill me first.

PHILIP. For your hospitable care,
Beauteous mountaineer, I would
That this ring's bright diamond could
Far outshine a star of air.

LUCY. Think me not a woman who
Lives intent her gain to make;
But I take it for your sake.

PAUL. (aside'. What I wonder should I do?
But if I'm her husband, then,
As I saw him give the ring,
Silence is the proper thing.

LUCY. In these arms I once again
Give to you my soul, for I
Have no other ring or chain.

PHILIP. Where I ever could remain: —

For such sweet captivity
Lures me from the miseries
Of remembering my sad fate,
Caused, as you have seen, so late,
By these crystalline blue seas.

PAUL (aside(. What! a new embrace! Halloo!
Don't you see, sir, Od's my life,
That this woman is my wife?

PHILIP. Here's your husband full in view;
He has seen us. I must straight
Leave you and return — (Aside.} Ah, me!
Couldst thou this, Polonia, see,
Thou mightst mourn, perhaps, the state
Unto which I see me doomed.
And. O heaven-aspiring sea,
Say in what vast depths can be
All the lives thou hast entombed?
(Exit.

## SCENE VI.

PAUL and LUCY; afterwards PHILIP.

PAUL (aside). As he's gone, I'll louder speak. —
This time, Lucy mine, I've caught you,
So a present I have brought you:
See this window-bar, 'twill wreak
My revenge.

LUCY. Oh, how malicious!
Bless me, grumbler, what grimaces!

PAUL. Then to witness two embraces
Does not look at all suspicious? —

Was it malice, then, in me,
Not plain seeing?

LUCY. Malice merely:
For a husband, how so nearly
He may pry, should never see
More than half his wife doth do.

PAUL. Well, with that I'm quite content,
To that condition I assent,
And since twice embraced by you
Has that rascal soldier been,
Whom the sea spewed out in spite,
I will juggle with my sight,
And pretend but once to have seen;
And as I for two embraces
Meant to give a hundred blows,
I but fifty now propose
For one half of my disgraces.
I have totted up the score;
You yourself the sentence gave;
Yes, by God I swear, you'll have
Fifty strokes and not one more.

LUCY. I've admitted far too much.
For a husband it would be
Quite preposterous; he should see
But the quarter.

PAUL. Even as such
I acknowledge the appeal.
Patience, and your back prepare,
For the now admitted share,
Five-and-twenty blows you'll feel.

LUCY. No, not so; you're still astray.

PAUL. Then say what?

LUCY. Between us two,
You're to trust not what you view,
But what I am pleased to say.

PAUL. Better far, I think, 'twould be,
Daughter of the devil, that you
Held the stick and used it too,
With it well belabouring me;
Is't agreed what I propose?
Yes; then let us both change places.
Give to him the two embraces,
And to me the hundred blows.

(PHILIP returns.

PHILIP (aside). Has the peasant gone, I wonder?

PAUL. At the nick of time you're here,
So, Sir Soldier, lend an ear.
Obligation I am under
For the favours you have meant
To bestow so liberally
On my cot, my wife, and me;
And although I'm well content
With you, yet as you're progressing
Day by day and getting stronger,
It is best you stay no longer.
Take the road, then, with God's blessing,
Leave my house, for it would be
Sad in it to raise my hand,
Leaving you dead flesh on land
Who wert living fish at sea.

PHILIP. The suspicion that you show
Is quite groundless, do not doubt it.

PAUL. Zounds! with reason or without it,
Am I married, sir, or no?

### SCENE VII.

LEOGAIRE, an Old Peasant, and PATRICK.

LEOGAIRE. So 'tis ordered, and that he
Serving here from day to day,
In the open field should stay.

OLD MAN. Yes; I say it so shall be.

LEOGAIRE. But who's this? O happiness!
Since 'tis Philip's form I greet.
Mighty lord, I kiss thy feet.

PAUL. Mighty lord does he call him?

LUCY. Yes.
Now lay on the blows you owe.
Now, friend Paul, the moment charms.

PHILIP. Give me, good Leogaire, your arms.

LEOGAIRE. Honour in them you bestow.
Is it possible, once more
That alive I see thee?

PHILIP. Here,
Trophy of a fate severe,
The sea flung me on this shore,
Where, their willing aid secured,

I have lived these peasants' guest,
Till I could repair with rest
All the sufferings I endured.
And, besides, I thought with dread
On the angry disposition
Of the king: for his ambition
When has it or bowed the head,
Or with patience heard related
The sad tragedies of fate?
Hopeless and disconsolate
In this solitude I've waited,
Till some happy chance might rise
When no longer I should grieve,
And the king would give me leave
To appear before his eyes.

LEOGAIRE. That already has been given thee;
For so sad was he, believing
Thou wert dead, so deep his grieving,
All the past will be forgiven thee
Since thou livest. Come with me,
Fortune will once more embrace thee, —
In his favour to replace thee
Let my happy privilege be.

PAUL. For that late unseemly brawl
See me humbly bending low;
You, my lord Prince Philip, know
That I am one Juan Paul.
My suspicion and abuse
Pray forgive, your majesty,
Think that what I said to thee
Was but cackled by a goose.
At your service, night and day,
Are whatever goods I've got —
Lucy here, myself and cot;

And God bless us all, I pray.

PHILIP. For your hospitality
I am grateful, and I trust
To repay it.

PAUL. If you must,
Let the first instalment be
Just to take my wife away.
Thurs you will reward us two;
She'll be glad to go with you,
I, without her, glad to stay.

(Exeunt PHILIP and LEOGAIRE.

LUCY (aside). Was there ever love so vain
As is mine, a brief caress
Cradled in forgetfulness?

OLD MAN. Juan Paul, as we remain
Here alone, 'twere well to greet
As a friend this labourer,
Newly sent us.

PATRICK. Nay, good sir,
I'm a slave, and I entreat
That as such you understand me;
I, the lowest of the low,
Hither come to serve, and so
I implore that you command me
As a slave, since I am one.

OLD MAN. Oh, what modesty!

PAUL. What humility!

LUCY. What good looks, too, and gentility!
I, in truth, can't help being drawn
By his face.

PAUL. Came ever here
(This is quite between us two)
Any wandering stranger who
Did not draw you so, my dear?
Eh, my Lucy?

LUCY. Boorish, base,
Is your vile insinuation
'Gains my innocent inclination
For the whole of the human race!
(Exit.

OLD MAN. To your sharpness and good will,
Paul, I trust a thing that may
Cost my life.

PAUL. Then don't delay.
Tell it, since you know my skill.

OLD MAN. This new slave that here you see,
I suspect is not secure,
And I hasten to procure
Means by which he more may be.
For the present I confide him
To your care, by day or night
Let him not escape your sight,
Ever watchful keep beside him.
(Exit.

# SCENE VIII.

PATRICK and PAUL.

PAUL (aside). I'm to keep what you discarded!
Good in faith! — (To PATRICK) Behold in me
Your strict guard; in you I see
The sole thing I ever guarded
In my life; with such a care
I can neither sleep nor eat.
If you wish to use your feet
You can go, your road lies there.
Nay, in flying quickly hence
You to me a good will do,
Since my care will fly with you.
Go in peace.

PATRICK. With confidence
You may trust me, for I'm not,
Though a slave, a fugitive.
Lord! how gladly do I live
In this solitary spot,
Where my soul in raptured prayer
May adore Thee, or in trance
See the living countenance
Of Thy prodigies so rare!
Human wisdom, earlthly lore,
Solitude reveals and reaches;
What diviner wisdom teaches
In it, too, I would explore.

PAUL. Tell me, talking thus apart,
Who it is on whom you call?

PATRICK. Great primeval cause of all,
Thou, O Lord, in all things art!

These blue heavens, these crystal skies
Formed of dazzling depths of light,
In which sun, moon, stars unite,
Are they not but draperies
Hung before Thy heavenly land? —
The discordant elements,
Water, fire, earth, air immense,
Prove they not Thy master hand?
Or in dark or brightsome hours,
Praise they not Thy power and might?
O'er the earth dost Thou not write
In the characters of flowers
Thy great goodness? And the air,
In reverberating thunder,
Does it not in fear and wonder
Say, O Lord, that Thou art there?
Are not, too, Thy praises sung
By the fire and water — each
Dowered for this divinest speech,
With tongue the wave, the flame with tongue?
Here, then, in this lonely place
I, O Lord, may better be,
Since in all things I find Thee.
Thou hast given to me the grace
Of Obedience, Faith, and Fear;
As a slave, then, let me stay,
Or remove me where I may
Serve Thee truly, if not here.

(An Angel descends, holding in one hand a shield in which is a mirror, and in the other hand a letter.

### SCENE IX.

An Angel. — THE SAME.

ANGEL. Patrick!

PATRICK. Ah! who calls me?

PAUL. Why,
No one calls. (Aside.) The man is daft,
Poetry should be his craft.

ANGEL. Patrick!

PATRICK. Ah! who calls me?

ANGEL. I.

PAUL (aside). Who he speaks to, I can't see.
Well, to stop his speech were hard,
I'm not here his mouth to guard.
(Exit.

### SCENE X.

The Angel and PATRICK.

PATRICK. Ah! it cannot be to me
Comes such glory! For, behold!
Pearl and rosy dawn in one,
Shines a cloud, from which its sun
Breaks in crimson and in gold!
Living stars its robe adorning,
Rose and jasmine sweetly blended,
Dazzling comes that vision splendid,
Scattering purple pomps of morning.

ANGEL. PATRICK!

PATRICK. Sunlight strikes me blind!

Heavenly Lord, who canst thou be?

ANGEL. I am Victor, whom to thee
God thy angel-guard assigned:
With this scroll, to give it thee
(Gives him the letter.
I am sent.

PATRICK. Sweet messenger,
Paranymph of all things fair,
Who amidst the hierarchy
Of the highest hosts of heaven
Singest in melodious tone —
"Glory unto Thee alone,
Holy, Holy Lord, be given!"

ANGEL. Read the letter.

PATRICK. With amaze,
I see here "To Patrick" Oh,
Can a slave be honoured so?

ANGEL. Open it.

PATRICK. It also says —
"Patrick! Patrick! hither come,
Free us from our slavery!" —
More it means than I can see,
Since I do not know by whom
I am called. Oh, faithful guide,
Speedily dispel my error!

ANGEL. Look into this shining mirror.

PATRICK. Heavens!

ANGEL. What seest thou inside?

PATRICK. Numerous people there seem thronging,
Old men, children, women, who
Seem to call me.

ANGEL. Nor do you
Stay, but satisfy their longing.
You behold the Irish nation,
Who expect to hear God's truth
From your lips. Oh, chosen youth,
Leave your slavery. The vocation
God has given thee is to sow
Faith o'er all the Irish soil.
There as Legate thou shalt toil,
Ireland's great Apostle. Go
First to France, to German's home,
The good bishop: there thou'lt make
Thy profession: there thou'lt take
The monk's habit, and to Rome
Pass, where letters thou'lt procure
For that mighty work of thine,
In the bulls of Celestine:
Thou wilt visit, then, in Tours
Martin, the great bishop there.
Now upborne upon the wind
Come with me, for thou wilt find
God has given with prescient care
His commands to all, that so
Fitly thy great work be done;
But 'tis time we should be gone:
Let us on our journey go.
(They disappear.

## ACT THE SECOND.

### HALL OF A TOWER IN THE PALACE OF EGERIUS.

#### SCENE I.

LUIS and POLONIA

LUIS. Yes, Polonia, yes, for he
Who betrays inconstancy
Has no reason for complaining
That another love is gaining
On his own; that fault will be
Ever punished so. For who
Proudly soars that doth not fall?
Therefore 'tis that I forestall
Philip's love howe'er so true.
He is nobler to the view,
As one nobly born may be;
But in that nobility,
Which one's self can win and wear,
I with justice may declare
I am nobler far than he;
I more honour have obtained
Than on Philip's cradle rained:
Let the fact excuse the boast,
For this land from coast to coast
Rings with victories I have gained.
Three years is it since I came
To these isles (it seems a day);
Three swift years have rolled away
Since I made it my chief aim
Thee to serve — my highest fame.
Trophies numerous as the sand,
Mars might envy, has my hand
Won for thy great sire and thee —

Being the wonder of the sea,
And th' amazement of the land.

POLONIA. Luis, yes, thy gallant bearing,
Or inherited or acquired,
Has within my breast inspired
A strange fear, a certain daring, —
Ah, I know not if, declaring
This, 'tis love, for blushes rise
At perceiving with surprise
That at last hath come the hour,
When my heart must own the power
Of a deity I despise.
This alone I'll say, that here
Long thy hope had been fruition,
But that I the disposition
Of the king, my father, fear,
But still hope and persevere.

## SCENE II.

PHILIP. — THE SAME.

PHILIP (aside). If to find my death I come,
Why precipitate my doom?
But so patient who could be
As to not desire to see
What impends, how dark its gloom?

LUIS. Then, what pledge may I demand
Of your faith?

POLONIA. This hand.

PHILIP. Not so,
How to hinder it I shall know;

More of this I must withstand.

POLONIA. Woe is me!

PHILIP. Wilt give thy hand
to this outcast of the wave?
And, oh thou, to whom pride gave
The presumption to aspire
To a sun's celestial fire,
Knowing that thou wert my slave,
Why thus dare to come between
Me and mine?

LUIS. Because I dare
Be what now I am, nor care
More to be what I have been.
It is true that I was seen
Once your slave: for who, indeed,
Can the fickle wheel control?
But in nobleness of soul
The best blood of all your breed
I can equal, nay, exceed.

PHILIP. Exceed ME? Vile homicide!
Wretch . . . .

LUIS. In having thus replied
You have made a slight mistake.

PHILIP. No.

LUIS. If such you did not make,
You've done worse.

PHILIP. Say, what?

LUIS. You've lied!

PHILIP. Villain! traitor
(Strikes him in the face.

POLONIA. Oh, ye skies!

LUIS. For so many injuries
Why not instant vengeance take,
When volcanic fires awake
In my breast, and hell-flames rise?
(They draw their swords.

## SCENE III.

EGERIUS and soldiers. — THE SAME.

KING. What is this?

LUIS. A lasting woe,
A misfortune, an abuse,
A sharp pain, a fiend let loose
From the infernal pit below.
Let no one presume to go
'Twixt me and revenge. Reflect,
Fury breathes immortal breath,
Vengeance has no fear of death,
Nor for any man respect.
I my honour must protect.

KING. Seize him.

LUIS. Let the man who sighs
For his death obey! You'll see
How the boldest fares, for he,
Even before your very eyes,

Shall be slain.

KING. That this should rise! —
Follow him.

LUIS. In desperate mood,
Plunging headlong in red blood,
Like a sea both wide and deep,
Thus courageously I leap,
Seeking Philip through the flood.

(All enter fighting.

## SCENE IV.

KING. I but wanted this alone
After what I've heard, that he
Who escaped from slavery,
And to distant Rome had flown,
Now with purpose too well known,
Has to Ireland come again,
Where proclaiming the new reign
Of the faith, he has enticed
Many to believe in Christ,
Rending all the world in twain.
A magician he must be,
Since condemned, so rumour saith,
By some other kings to death,
He though tied upon the tree
In an instant set him free,
With such prodigies of wonder
That the earth (within whose womb
The dead lie as in a tomb)
Trembled, the air groaned in thunder,
Dark eclipse the sun lay under,
Deigning not a single glance

Of his radiant countenance
To the moon: from which I see
That this Patrick, for 'tis he,
Lords it over fate and chance;
Awe-struck by the prodigy,
Fearing they may punished be,
Crowds attend him on his way.
And 'tis said that he to-day
Comes to try his spells on me.
Let him come, and once for all
Wave in vain his conjuring rod!
We shall see who is this God,
Whom their God the Christians call.
By my hand must Patrick fall,
Were it but to see if he
Can escape his destiny,
Or my will subvert and master,
He this Bishop, he this Pastor,
He Pope's Legate, though he be.

## SCENE V.

The Captain, Soldiers, LUIS a prisoner, The King.

CAPTAIN. Luis, sire, without delay
We secured; but not before
He killed three, and wounded more,
Of our company.

KING. Christian, say,
Why do you no fear display,
Seeing now in angry mood
My hand raised to shed your blood?
But in vain do I deplore,
Since he this deserves and more
Who has done a Christian good.

Gifts, not chastisement, should be
Thine to-day, for it is plain
It is I should feel the pain
For conferring good on thee.
Take him hence, and presently
Let him die; and be it known
Why from him has mercy flown.
'Tis not for his crimes or guilt
That this Christian's blood is spilt,
'Tis for Christ's belief alone.
(*Exeunt.*

## SCENE VI.

LUIS.

LUIS. If for this I die, to me
Thou the happiest death allottest,
Since he for his God will die,
He who dies to do Him honour.
And a man whose life is here
But a round of cares and crosses,
Should be grateful unto death
As the end of all his sorrows;
Since it comes the tangled thread
Of a wretched life to shorten,
Which to-day the evil Phoenix
Of its works that now prove mortal
Would revive amid the ashes
Of my wrong and my dishonour.
Then my life, my breath were poison,
Venom would my breast but foster,
Until I had shed in Ireland
Blood in such a copious torrent,
That though base it might wash out
The remembrance of my wronger.

Ah, my honour, low thou liest,
By a ruthless foot down trodden! —
I will die with thee, united
We two will together conquer
These barbarians. Then since little,
But a span at best, belongeth
To my life, a noble vengeance
Let this dagger take upon me! —
But, good God! what evil impulse
With demoniac instinct prompteth
Thus my hand? I am a Christian,
I've a soul, and share the godly
Light of faith: then were it right,
'Mid a crowd of Gentile mockers,
Thus the Christian faith to tarnish
By an action so improper?
What example would I give them
By a death so sad and shocking,
Save that I thus gave the lie
To the works that Patrick worketh.
Since they'd say, who worship only
Their own vices most immodest,
Who deny unto the soul
Its eternal joy or torment,
"Of what use is Patrick's preaching
That man's soul must be immortal,
If the Christian, Luis Enius,
Kills himself? He can't acknowledge
Its eternal life who'd lose it." —
Thus with actions so discordant,
He the light and I the shadow,
We would neutralize each other.
'Tis enough to be so wicked
As even now to feel no sorrow,
No repentance for past sins,
Rather a desire for others.

Yes, by God! for if escape
Fortune now my life would offer,
Europe, Africa, and Asia
I would fill with fear and horror;
First exacting here the debt
Of a vengeance so enormous,
That these islands of Egerius
Would not hold a single mortal
Who should not appease the thirst,
The insatiable longing
That I have for blood. The lightning,
When it bursts its prison portals,
Warns us in a voice of thunder,
And then 'twixt dark smoke and forked
Fires that take the shape of serpents,
Fills the trembling air with horror.
I, too, gave that thunder voice,
So that all men heard the promise,
But the lightning bolt was wanting.
Yes, ah me! it proved abortive,
And before it touched the earth
Was by dallying winds made sport of.
No, it is not death that grieves me,
Even a death of such dishonour,
'Tis because at last are ended,
In my youth's fresh opening blossom,
My offences. Life I wish for
To begin from this day forward
Greater and more dread excesses.
Heavens! 'tis for no other object.

## SCENE VII.

POLONIA. — LUIS.

POLONIA (aside) (Now with mind made up I come.)

Luis, an occasion offers
Ever as the test and touchstone
Of true love. By certain knowledge
Have I learned the imminent danger
Of thy life. The wrath grows hotter
Of my father, and his fury
To evade is most important.
All the guards that here are with thee
Has my liberal hand suborned,
So that at the clink of gold
Have their ears grown deaf and torpid.
Fly! and that thou mayest see
How a woman's heart can prompt her,
How her honour she can trample,
How her self-respect leave prostrate,
With thee I will go, since now
It is needful that henceforward
I in life and death am thine,
For without thee life were worthless,
Thou who in my heart dost live.
I bring with me gems and money
Quite enough to the most distant
Parts of India to transport us,
Where the sun with beams and shadows
Scatters frost, or burning scorches.
At the door two steeds are standing,
I should rather call these horses
Two swift lynxes, air-born creatures,
Thoughts by liveliest minds begotten;
They so rapid are, that though
We as fugitives fly on them,
An assurance of our safety
We shall feel. At once resolve then.
Why thus ponder? what delays thee?
Time is pressing, therefore shorten
All discourse; and that mischance,

Which disturbs love's plans so often,
May not offer an obstruction
To so well-prepared a project,
First before thee I will go.
Issue, while in specious converse
I divert thy guards, and give
To thy coming forth a cover.
Even the sun our project favours,
Which amid the west waves yonder,
Sinking, dips his golden curls
To refresh his glowing forehead.
(Exit.

## SCENE VIII.

LUIS.

LUIS. A most opportune occasion
To my hands has fortune offered;
Since Heaven knows that all the show
Of apparent love and fondness
Which I proffered to Polonia
Was assumed, it being my object
She should go with me, where I,
Seizing on the gold and costly
Gems she carries, so might issue
From this Babylonian bondage.
For although in my person
Was esteemed and duly honoured,
Still 'twas slavery after all,
And my free wild life was longing
For that liberty, heaven's best gift,
Which I had enjoyed so often.
But a great embarrassment
And a hindrance were a woman
For the end I have in view,

Since in me is love a folly
That ne'er passes appetite,
Which being satisfied, no longer
Care I for a woman's presence,
How so fair or so accomplished.
And since thus my disposition
Is so free, of what importance
Is a murder more or less?
At my hands must die Polonia
For her loving at a time
When there's no one loved or honoured.
Had she loved as others love,
Then she would have lived as others.
(Exit.

## SCENE IX.

The Captain; then The King, PHILIP, and LEOGAIRE.

CAPTAIN. The sad sentence of his death
Have I come, by the king's orders,
Here to read to Luis Enius. —
But what's this? The door lies open,
And the tower deserted. Ha!
Soldiers! No one answers. Ho, there!
Guards, come hither, treason! treason!

(Enter The King, PHILIP, and LEOGAIRE.

KING. Why these outcries? this commotion?
What is this?

CAPTAIN. That Luis Enius
Has escaped, and from the fortress
All the guards have fled.

LEOGAIRE. My lord,
I saw entering here Polonia.

PHILIP. Heavens! beyond all doubt 'twas she
Who released him. That her lover
He dared call him, you well know.
Jealousy and rage provoke me
To pursue them. A new Troy
Will to-day be Ireland's story.
(Exit.

KING. Give me, too, a horse; in person
I these fugitives will follow.
Ah, what Christians are these two
Who with actions so discordant,
One deprives me of my rest,
And the other robs my honour?
But the twain shall feel the weight
Of my vengeful hands fall on them;
For not safe from me would be
Even their sovereign Roman Pontiff.
(Exeunt.

## SCENE X.

A WOOD, AT WHOSE EXTREMITY IS PAUL'S CABIN.

POLONIA flying wounded, and LUIS with a naked dagger in his hand.

POLONIA. Oh, hold thy bloody hand!
Though love be dead, let Christian faith command.
My honour take; but, oh, my poor life spare,
That suppliant at thy feet pours out its humble prayer.

LUIS. Hapless Polonia, since creation's hour

Beauty has ever one unvarying dower,
It brings misfortune with it, it is this
Makes beauty rarely live long time with bliss.
I, who less pity feel
Than any headsman who e'er held death's steel,
May by thy death procure
My life, since with it I will go secure.
If thee I bring where fortune's hand may guide me
I bring the witness of my woes beside me,
By whom they may pursue me,
Track me, discover me, in fact, undo me
If here I leave thee living,
I leave thee angry, vengeful, unforgiving;
Leave thee, in fact, to be
One enemy more (and what an enemy!);
Thus equally I grieve thee,
Thus evil do whether I take or leave thee;
And so 'tis better thus,
That I a wretch, cruel and infamous,
False, impious, fierce, abandoned, wicked, banned
By God and man, should slay thee by my hand,
Since buried here,
Within the rustic entrails dark and drear
Of this rude realm of stone,
My worst misfortune shall remain unknown.
My fury, too, shall gain
A novel kind of vengeance when thou'rt slain,
Remaining satisfied
That Philip, too, by the same stroke has died,
If in thy heart he lived; and then mine ire
Will need no victim more except thy sire.
Through thee first came
My first disgrace, the cause of all my shame,
And so the first of all
On thee my vengeful strokes shall furious fall.

POLONIA. Ah me! my fate pursuing,
I have but only worked my own undoing,
Like to the worm that by its subtle art
Spins its own grave. Hast thou a human heart?

LUIS. I am a demon. So to prove it, die.
Thus —

POLONIA. God of Patrick, listen to my cry!

(He stabs her several times, and she falls within.

LUIS. She fell on flowers, there sowing
Both lives and horrors in her blood outflowing.
Thus now with greater ease
I can escape, and carry o'er the seas,
In many a gem and chain,
Treasure enough to make me rich in Spain,
Until so changed by time,
Disguised by wandering in a foreign clime,
I may return to reap
My vengeance; for a wrong doth never sleep.
But whither do I stray,
Treading the shades of death in this dark way?
My path is lost: I go
Whither I do not know;
Perchance escaping from my prison bands
To fall again into my tyrant's hands.
If the dark night doth not my sight deceive,
Yonder a rustic cabin I perceive.
Yes, I am right. I'll knock; I can't much err,
They'll know the way.
(He knocks.

## SCENE XI.

PAUL and LUCY. — LUIS.

LUCY (within). Who's there?

LUIS. A traveller,
Benighted, his way lost, confused, distressed,
Good worthy husbandman, disturbs thy rest.

LUCY (within). Ho, Juan! how you snore!
Awake! there's some one knocking at the door.

PAUL (within). Why, I am well enough here in my bed.
He knocks for you, so answer him instead.

LUCY (within). Who's there?

LUIS. A traveller, I say.

PAUL (within). A traveller?

LUIS. Yes.

PAUL (within). Then travel on, I pray.
This cabin is no inn, sir, not a bit.

LUIS. I'm getting weary of this fellow's wit.
I'll try what kicking in the door will do.
(Drives in the door.
Ay, there it goes.

LUCY (within). Why, Juan Paul, halloo!
Awake, I say, for if I don't mistake,
The door's knocked in.

PAUL (within). Well, one eye is awake,
But underneath its lid the other's laid. —
Come with me, Lucy, for I'm sore afraid.

(Enter PAUL and LUCY.
Who's there?

LUIS. Be silent, peasants, and attend
If you would not that now your lives should end.
Lost in this woodland waste
I sought your door; and so, my friend, make haste
To tell me the best way
From this to the port, where I by break of day
May from the coast get clear.

PAUL. Go right ahead: first take the pathway here,
They left, then right again,
Rise where there's hill, descend where there's a plain,
And going thus, in short,
The port you'll reach when you have reached the port.

LUIS. 'Tis better that you come
Along with me, or by the heavens o'erhead,
Your blood shall stain the ground on which you tread.

LUCY. Were it not better, cavalier,
To pass the night here till the dawn appear?

PAUL. How very kind you are when least expected!
Are you already to this knight infected?

LUIS. Choose now, at once, I say,
To die or guide me.

PAUL. Don't be vexed, I pray;
If I without more haggling or vain clack

Select to go, and carry you on my back,
If so you chose, 'tis not that death I fear,
But just to disappoint my Lucy here.

LUIS (aside). That he may not betray
Whither I go, to those who track my way,
Him from some cliff I'll throw
Headlong amid the icy waves below. —
(To LUCY.
You with this consolation here remain
Your husband will be with you soon again.
(Exeunt the two at one side, and she at the other.

## SCENE XII.

The King EGERIUS, LESBIA, LEOGAIRE, The Captain;
afterwards PHILIP.

LESBIA. Not a trace of them is found;
All the mountain, hill and valley,
Leaf by leaf has been explored,
Bough by bough has been examined,
Rock by rock has been searched through,
Still no clue wherewith to track them
Can we light on.

KING. Without doubt,
To preserve them from my anger,
Has the earth engulphed the two;
For not heaven itself could guard them
From my wrath if still they lived.

LESBIA. See the sun his disentangled
Golden tresses far extends
Over mountains, groves and gardens,
Showing that the day hath come.

(Enter PHILIP.
PHILIP. Deign, your majesty, to hearken
To a tragedy more dreadful,
To a crime more unexampled
Than has time or fortune ever
Yet recorded in earth's annals.
Seeking traces of Polonia
Through these savage woods distracted
Roamed I restless all the night-time,
Till at length and amid the darkness
Half awakened rose the dawn;
Not in veils of gold and amber
Was she dressed, a robe of mourning
Formed of clouds composed her mantle,
And with discontented light
Hidden were the stars and planets,
Though for this one time alone
They were happy in their absence.
Searching there in every part,
We approached where blood was spattered
On the tender dewy flower,
And upon the ground some fragments of a woman's dress were strewn.
By these signs at once attracted,
We went on, 'till at the foot
Of a great rock overhanging,
In a fragrant tomb of roses
Lay Polonia, dead and stabbed there.

## SCENE XIII.

POLONIA dead; and afterwards PATRICK. — THE SAME.

PHILIP. Turn your eyes, and here you see
The young tree of beauty blasted,

Pale and sad the opening flower,
The bright flame abruptly darkened;
See here loveliness laid prostrate,
See warm life here turned to marble,
See, alas! Polonia dead.

KING. Philip, cease! proceed no farther!
For I have not resignation
To bear up with any calmness
'Gainst so many forms of wrong,
'Gainst so many shapes of sadness,
'Gainst such manifold misfortunes.
Ah, my daughter! Ah, thou hapless
Treasure fatally found for me!

LESBIA. Grief my feeling so o'ermasters
That I have not breath to mourn.
Ah! of all thy woes the partner
Let thy wretched sister be!

KING. What rude hand in ruffian anger
Raised its bloody steel against
Beauty so divinely fashioned?
Sorrow, sorrow ends my life.

PATRICK (within). Woe to thee, sin-stained Irlanda!
Woe to thee, unhappy people!
If with tears thou dost not water
The hard earth, and night and day
Weeping in thy bitter anguish,
Ope the golden gates of heaven
Which thy disobedience fastened.
Woe to thee, unhappy people!
Woe to thee, sin-stained Irlanda!

KING. Heavens! what mournful tones are these?

What are these sad solemn accents
That transpierce my very heart,
That cut through me like a dagger?
Learn who thus disturbs the flowing
Of my grief's most tender channels.
Who but I should so lament?
Who but I should wail thus sadly?

LEOGAIRE. This, my lord, is Patrick, who
Having as you know, departed
From this country went to Rome,
Where the Pontiff, the great father,
Made him bishop, and a post
Of pre-eminence imparted
To him here; through all the islands
He proceedeth in this manner.

(PATRICK enters.

PATRICK. Woe to thee, unhappy people!
Woe to thee, sin-stained Irlanda!

KING. Patrick, thou who thus my grief
Interrupted, and my sadness
Doubled with thy golden words,
Hiding false and poisonous matter,
Why thus persecute me? Wherefore
Thus disturb the hills and valleys
Of my kingdom with deceptions
And new-fangled laws and maxims?
Here we know but this alone,
We are born and die. Our fathers
Left us this, the simple doctrine
Taught by nature, and no farther
Have we sought to learn. What God
Can be this, of whom such marvels

You relate, who life eternal
Gives when temporal life departeth?
Can the soul, when it is severed
From the body, be so active
As to have another life,
Or of bale or bliss, hereafter?

PATRICK. Being loosened from the body,
And the human portion having
Given to nature, it being only
But a little dust and ashes,
Then the spirit upward rises,
To the higher sphere attracted,
Where its labours find their centre,
If it dies in grace, which baptism
First confers upon the soul,
And then penance ever after.

KING. Then this beauteous one, that here
Lies in her own blood bedabbled,
There, is living at this moment?

PATRICK. Yes.

KING. A sign, a proof, then, grant me
Of this truth.

PATRICK (aside). Almighty Lord!
For Thy glory deign to hearken!
It behoveth Thee to show
Here Thy power by an example.

KING. What! you do not answer?

PATRICK. Heaven
Wishes for itself to answer. —

In the name of God, O corse,
(He extends his hands over the dead body of POLONIA.
Lying stiff here, I command thee
To arise and live, resuming
Thine own soul, and thus make patent
This great truth, before us preaching
The true doctrine and evangel.

POLONIA (arising). Woe is me! Oh, save me, heaven!
Ah, what secrets are imparted
To the soul! O Lord! O Lord!
Stay the red hand of Thy anger,
Of Thy justice. Do not threaten,
'Gainst a woman weak and abject,
The dread thunders of Thy rigour,
Of Thy power the lightning's flashes.
Where, oh, where shall I conceal me
From Thy countenance, if haply
Thou art wroth? Ye rocks, he mountains,
Fall upon and overcast me.
Hating mine own self, to-day
Would that to my prayer 'twas granted
In the centre of the earth
From Thy sight to hide and mask me!
Ah, but why? if wheresoever
My unhappy fate might cast me
There I brought with me my sin?
See ye, see ye not this Atlas
Back recede, and this huge mountain
Tremble to its base? The axes
Of the firmament are loosened,
And its perfect fabric hangeth
Threatening ruin o'er my head,
With terrific pride and grandeur.
Darker grows the air around me,
Chained, my feet proceed no farther,

Even the seas retire before me.
What, here fly me not nor startle,
Are the wild beasts, which to rend me
Bit by bit come on to attack me.
Mercy, mighty Lord, oh, mercy!
Pardon, gracious Lord, oh, pardon!
Holy baptism I implore,
That in grace I may depart hence.
Mortals, hear, oh, mortals hear,
Christ is living, Christ is master,
Christ is god, the one true God!
Penance, penance, penance practice!
(Exit.

## SCENE XIV.

THE SAME, with the exception of POLONIA.

PHILIP. How prodigious!

CAPTAIN. How stupendous!

LESBIA. What a miracle!

LEOGAIRE. What a marvel!

KING. What enchantment! what bewitchment!
Who can bear this? who can grant this?

ALL. Christ is God, the one true God.

KING. What a bold deceit is practised
Here, blind people, to deceive you,
In the making of these marvels,
Which you have not sense to see
Are in outward show but acted

And within are fraud! However,
That the truth be now established,
I will own myself convinced,
If in argument shall Patrick
Prove his case: and so attend
As the grave dispute advances.
If the soul was made immortal
It could never be inactive
Even for a single moment.

PATRICK. Yes; and every dream that passes
Proves this truth; because the dreams
That engender numerous phantoms
Are discourses of the soul
That ne'er sleeps, and as these shadows
Simulate the imperfect actions
Of the senses, a strange language
And imperfect is produced;
And 'tis thus that in their trances
Men dream things that are at once
Inconsistent and fantastic.

KING. Well, then, this being so, I ask
Was Polonia when this happened
Dead or not? For if but only
In a swoon, what mighty marvel,
Then, was done? But this I pass.
If she really had departed,
Then to one of the two places,
Heaven or hell, so named, O Patrick,
By yourself, it must have gone.
If it was in heaven, 'twas hardly
Merciful in God to send it
Back into this world, to hazard
A new chance of condemnation,
When 'twas once in grace and happy.

This is surely true. If, likewise,
It had been in hell, 'tis adverse
To strict justice, since it were not
Just that that which by its badness
Once had earned such punishment,
Should again be given the chances
Of regaining grace. It must,
I presume, be taken as granted
That God's justice and His mercy
Cannot possibly be parted.
Where, I ask then, was her soul?

PATRICK. Hear, Egerius, the answer.
I concede that for the soul,
Sanctified by holy baptism,
Heaven or hell must be its goal,
Out of which, by God's commandment,
Speaking of His usual power,
It can never more be absent.
But if of His absolute power
There is question, God could drag it
Even from hell itself; but this
Is not what we have to argue.
That the soul doth go to either
Of those places, must be granted
When 'tis severed from the body
Once for all by mortal absence
To return to it no more;
But when otherwise commanded
To it to return, it waiteth
In a certain state of passage,
And remains as 'twere suspended
In the universe, not having
Any special place allotted.
For the Almighty mind forecasting
All things, when from out His essence,

As th' exemplar, the fair pattern
Of His thought, this glorious fabric
He brought forth to light and gladness,
Saw this very incident,
And well knowing what would happen,
That this soul would here return,
Kept it for awhile inactive,
Seemingly unfixed, yet fixed.
This is the authentic answer
That theology, that sacred
Science, gives to what you have asked me.
But another point remaineth:
There are other places, mark me,
Both of glory and of pain,
Than you think; and of these latter
One is called the Purgatory,
Where the soul of him who haply
Dies in grace, is purged from stains,
Sinful stains which it contracted
In the world: for into heaven
None can pass till these are cancelled.
And thus, there 'tis purified,
Cleansed by fire from all that tarnished,
Till to God's divinest presence
Pure and clean at length it passes.

KING. So you say, and I have nothing
To confirm what you advance here
But your word. Some proof now give me,
Give me something I can handle,
Something tangible to convince me
Of this truth, that I may grasp it,
And know what it is. And since
So much power and influence have you
With your God, implore His grace,
That I may believe the faster,

Some material fact to give me,
Something that we all can grapple,
Not mere creatures of the mind.
And remember that at farthest
But an hour remains in which
You must give me sure and ample
Signs of punishment and glory,
Or you die. These mighty marvels
Of your God here let them come,
Where the truth we can examine
For ourselves. And if we neither
Heaven or hell deserve to have here,
Show us, then, this Purgatory,
Which is different from the latter,
So that here we all may know
His omnipotence and grandeur.
Mind, God's honour rests upon you,
Tell Him to defend and guard it.
(*Exeunt all but* PATRICK.

## SCENE XV.

PATRICK.

PATRICK. Here, mighty Lord, dart down thy searching glance,
Arm'd with the dreadful lightnings of Thine ire,
Wing'd with Thy vengeance, as the bolt with fire,
And rout the squadrons of fell ignorance:
Come not in pity to the hostile band,
Treat not as friends Thy enemies abhorr'd,
But since they ask for portents, mighty Lord,
Come with the blood-red lightnings in Thy hand.
Of old Elias asked with burning sighs
For chastisement, and Moses did display
Wonders and portents; in the self-same way
Listen, O Lord, to my beseeching cries,

And though I be not great or good as they,
Still let my accents pierce the listening skies!
Portents and chastisement, both day and night
I ask, O Lord, may from Thy hand be given,
That Purgatory, Hell and Heaven,
May be revealed unto these mortals' sight.

## SCENE XVI.

A Good Angel at one side, and on the other a Bad Angel. — PATRICK.

BAD ANGEL (to himself). Fearful that the favouring skies
May accede to Patrick's prayer,
And discover to him where
Earth's most wondrous treasure lies,
Like a minister of light,
Full of scorn, I hither fly
It to chill and nullify.
Covering with my poison blight
His petition.

GOOD ANGEL. Then give o'er,
Cruel monster; for in me
His protecting angel see.
But be silent, speak no more. —
(to him.
Patrick, God has heard Thy prayer,
He has listen'd to thy vows,
And, as thou hast asked, allows
Earth's great secrets to lie bare.
Seek along this island ground
For a vast and darksome cave,
Which restrains the lake's dark wave.
And supports the mountains round;
He who dares to go therein,

Having first contritely told
All his faults, shall there behold
Where the soul is purged from sin.
He shall see, with mortal eyes,
Hell itself, where those who die
In their sins for ever lie
In the fire that never dies.
He shall see, in blest fruition,
Where the happy spirits dwell.
But of this be sure as well —
He who without due contrition
Enters there to idly try
What the cave may be, doth go
To his death; he'll suffer woe,
While the Lord doth reign on high,
Who thy soul this day shall free
From this poor world's weariness.
It is thus that God doth bless
Those who love His name like thee.
He shall grant to thee in pity,
Bliss undreamed by mortal men,
Making thee a denizen
Of His own celestial city.
He shall to the world proclaim
His omnipotence and glory,
By the wondrous Purgatory
Which shall bear thy sainted name.
Lest thou think the promise vain
Of this miracle divine,
I will take this shape malign,
Which came hither to profane
Thy devotion, and within
This dark cavern's dark abyss
Fling it, — there to howl and hiss
In the everlasting din.
(*They disappear.*

PATRICK. Glory, glory unto Thee,
Mighty Lord; the heavens proclaim,
Miracles attest Thy name,
Wonders show that Thou must be. —
(Calling.
King!

SCENE XVII.

The King, PHILIP, LESBIA, LEOGAIRE, The Captain, People.
— PATRICK.

KING. What would'st thou?

PATRICK. Come with me
Through this mountain woodland drear,
Thou and all thy followers here,
Thou and they shall see therein
The dark place reserved for sin,
And rewards delightful sphere.
They shall have a passing view
Of a sight no tongue can tell,
An unending miracle,
To whose greatness shall be due
Their amazement ever new
Who its secrets shall unveil.
Yes, a perfect image pale
In the wonders guarded here,
Shall they see with awe and fear,
Of the realms of bliss and bale.
(Exit, followed by all.

# SCENE XVIII.

A REMOTE PART OF THE MOUNTAIN WITH THE MOUTH OF A HORRIBLE CAVE.

THE SAME.

KING. Look, O Patrick, for you go
Turning towards a part forbidden,
Where the light of the sun is hidden
Even in the noon-tide's glow.
Through this wilderness of woe
Even the hunter in pursuit
Of his prey ne'er placed a foot
On its trackless wild walks green,
Since for ages it has been
Shunned alike by man and brute.

PHILIP. We for many and many a year,
Who have lived here from our youth,
Never dared to learn the truth
Of the secrets hidden here;
For the entrance did appear
In itself enough to make
Even the bravest heart to quake.
No one yet has dared to brave
The wild rocks that guard this cave,
Or the waters of this lake.

KING. And for auguries we heard,
Borne the troubled wind along,
Oft the sad funereal song
Of some lone nocturnal bird.

PHILIP. Be the rash attempt deferred.

PATRICK. Let not causeless fear arise;
For a treasure of the skies
Here is hidden.

KING. What is fear?
Could it ever me come near
In an earthquake's agonies?
No; for though the flames should break
As from some sulphureous lake,
And the mountains' sides run red
From the molten fires outshed,
They could ne'er my courage shake,
Never make me fear.

## SCENE XIX.

POLONIA. — THE SAME.

POLONIA. Oh, stay,
Wandering from the path astray,
Hapless crowd, rash, indiscreet,
Turn away your erring feet,
For misfortune lies that way.

Here from myself with hurried footsteps flying,
I dared to treat this wilderness profound,
Beneath the mountain whose proud top defying
The pure bright sunbeam is with huge rocks crowned,
Hoping that here, as in its dark grave lying,
Never my sin could on the earth be found,
And I myself might find a port of peace
Where all the tempests of the world might cease.

No polar star had hostile fate decreed me,
As on my perilous path I dared to stray,
So great its pride, no hand presumed to lead me,

And guide my silent footstep on its way.
Not yet the aspect of the place has freed me
From the dread terror, anguish and dismay,
Which were awakened by this mountain's gloom,
And all the hidden wonders of its womb.

See ye not here this rock some power secureth,
That grasps with awful toil the hill-side brown,
And with the very anguish it endureth
Age after age seems slowly coming down?
Suspended there with effort, it obscureth
A mighty cave beneath, which it doth crown; —
An open mouth the horrid cavern shapes,
Wherewith the melancholy mountain gapes.

This, then, by mournful cypress trees surrounded,
Between the lips of rocks at either side,
Reveals a monstrous neck of length unbounded,
Whose tangled hair is scantily supplied
By the wild herbs that there the wind hath grounded,
A gloom whose depths no sun has ever tried,
A space, a void, the gladsome day's affright,
The fatal refuge of the frozen night.

I wished to enter there, to make my dwelling
Within the cave; but here my accents fail,
My troubled voice, against my will rebelling.
Doth interrupt so terrible a tale. —
What novel horror, all the past excelling,
Must I relate to you, with cheeks all pale,
Without cold terror on my bosom seizing,
And even my voice, my breath, my pulses freezing?

I scarcely had o'ercome my hesitation,
And gone within the cavern's vault profound,
When I heard wails of hopeless lamentation,

Despairing shrieks that shook the walls around,
Curses, and blasphemy, and desperation,
Dark crimes avowed that would even hell astound,
Which heaven, I think, in order not to hear,
Had hid within this prison dark and drear.

Let him come here who doubts what I am telling,
Let him here bravely enter who denies,
Soon shall he hear the sounds of dreadful yelling,
Soon shall the horrors gleam before his eyes.
For me, my voice is hushed, my bosom swelling,
Pants now with terror, now with strange surprise.
Nor is it right that human tongue should dare
High heaven's mysterious secrets to lay bare.

PATRICK. This cave, O king, which here you see, concealeth
The mysteries of life as well as death:
Not, I should say, for him whose bosom feeleth
No true repentance, or no real faith;
But he who boldly enters, who revealeth
His sins, confessing them with penitent breath,
Shall see them all forgiven, his conscience clear,
And have alive his Purgatory here.

KING. And dost thou think, O Patrick, that I owe
My blood so little, as to yield to dread,
And trembling fear like a weak woman show?
Say, who shall be the first this cave to tread?
What silent! Philip?

PHILIP. Sire, I dare not go.

KING. Then, Captain, thou?

CAPTAIN. Enough to strike me dead
Is even the thought.

KING. Leogaire, thou'lt surely dare?

LEOGAIRE. The heavens, my lord, themselves exclaim forbear!

KING. O cowards, lost to every sense of shame,
Unfit to gird the warrior's sword around
Your shrinking loins! Men are ye but in name.
Well, I myself shall be the first to sound
The depths of this enchantment, and proclaim
Unto this Christian that my heart unawed
Nor dreads his incantations nor his God!
(Egerius advances to the cave, and on entering sinks into it with much noise, flames rise from below, and many voices are heard.

POLONIA. How terrible!

LEOGAIRE. How awful!

PHILIP. What a wonder!

CAPTAIN. The earth is breathing out its central fire.
(Exit.

LEOGAIRE. The axes of the sky are burst asunder.
(Exit.

POLONIA. The heavens are loosening their collected ire.
{Exit.

LESBIA. The earth doth quake, and peals the sullen thunder.
(Exit.

PATRICK. O, mighty Lord, who will not now admire
Thy wondrous works?
(Exit.

PHILIP. Oh! who that's not insane
Will enter Patrick's Purgatory again?
(Exit.

## ACT THE THIRD.

A STREET. IT IS NIGHT.

### SCENE I.

JUAN PAUL, dressed ridiculously as a soldier, and LUIS ENIUS, very pensive.

PAUL. Yes, the day would come I knew,
After long procrastination,
When a word of explanation
I should ask to have with you.
"Come with me," you said. Though dark,
Off I trudged with heavy heart
To point out to you the part
Where at morn you could embark;
Then again, with thundering voice,
Thus you spoke, "Where I must fly
Choose to come with me, or die."
And, since you allowed a choice,
Of two ills I chose the worst,
Which, sir, was to go with you.
As your shadow then I flew
'Cross the sea to England first,
Then to Scotland, then to France
then to Italy and Spain,
Round the world and back again,
As in some fantastic dance.
Not a country great or small
Could escape you, 'till, good lack!

Here we are in Ireland back: —
Now, sir, I, plain Juan Paul,
Being perplexed to know what draws
You here now, with beard and hair
Grown so long, your speech, your air,
Changed so much, would ask the cause
Why you these disguises wear?
You by day ne'er leave the inn,
But when cold night doth begin
You a thousand follies dare,
Without bearing this in mind,
That we now are in a land
Wholly changed from strand to strand,
Where, in fact, we nothing find
As we left it. The old king
Died despairing, and his heir,
Lesbia, now the crown doth wear,
For her sister, hapless thing!
Poor Polonia . . . .

LUIS. Oh, that name
Do not mention! do not kill me
By repeating what doth thrill me
To the centre of my frame
As with lightning. Yes, I know
That at length Polonia died.

PAUL. Yes; our host was at her side
(He himself has told me so)
When they found her dead, and . . . .

LUIS. Cease!
Of her death, oh! speak no more,
'Tis sufficient to deplore,
And to pray that she's at peace.

PAUL. Leaving heathen sin and crime,
All the people far and near
Are become good Christians here.
For one Patrick, who some time
Now is dead . . . .

LUIS. Is Patrick dead?

PAUL. So I from our host have heard.

LUIS (aside). Badly have I kept my word! —
But proceed.

PAUL. The teaching spread
Of the faith of Christ, and gave,
As a proof complete and whole
Of the eternity of the soul,
The discovery of a cave. —
Oh! it's the very name doth send
Terror through me.

LUIS. Yes, I have heard
Of that cave, and every word
Made my hair to stand on end.
Those who in the neighbourhood
Dwell, see wonders every day.

PAUL. Since, 'mid terror and dismay,
In your melancholy mood
You will no one hear or see,
Ever locked within your room,
It is plain you have not come
Aught to learn, how strange they be,
Of these things. It doth appear
Other work you are about.
Satisfy my foolish doubt,

And say why we have come here.

LUIS. to your questions thus I yield:
Yes, I forced you, as you mention,
From your house, and my intention
Was to kill you in the field;
But I thought it best instead
You to make my steps attend
As my comrade and my friend,
Shaking off the mortal dread
Which forbad me to endure
Any stranger, and in fine,
That your arms being joined with mine,
I might feel the more secure.
Many a land, both far and near,
Passing through you fared right well;
And now answering I will tell
Why it is that we come here.
And 'tis this: I come to slay
Here a man who did me wrong,
'Tis for this I pass along,
Muffled in this curious way,
Hiding country, dress, and name;
And the night suits best for me,
For my powerful enemy
Can the first position claim
In the land. Since I avow
Why I hither have been led,
Listen now how I have sped
In my project until now.
I three days ago was brought
To this city in disguise,
For two nights, beneath the skies,
I my enemy have sought
In his street and at his door;
Twice a muffled figure came

And disturbed me in my aim,
Twice he called and stalked before
Him I followed in the street;
But when I the figure neared,
Suddenly he disappeared
As if wings were on his feet.
I this third night have brought you,
That should this mysterious shape
Come again, he sha'nt escape,
Being caught between us two;
Who he is we then can see.

PAUL. Two? who are they?

LUIS. You and I.

PAUL. I'm not one.

LUIS. Not one? How? Why?

PAUL. No, sir, no. I cannot be
One, nor half a one. These stories
Faith! would frighten fifty Hectors;
What know I of Lady Spectres,
Or of Lord Don Purgatories?
All through life I've kept aloof
From the other world's affairs,
Shunning much superfluous cares;
But, my courage put to proof,
Bid me face a thousand men,
And if I don't cut and run
From the thousand, nay, from one,
Never trust to me again.
For I think it quite a case
Fit for Bedlam, if so high,
That a man would rather die,

Than just take a little race.
Such a trifle! Sir, to me
Life is precious; leave me here,
Where you'd find me, never fear.

LUIS. Here's the house; to-night I'll be,
Philip, your predestined fate.
Now we'll see if heaven pretends
To defend him, and defends. —
Watch here, you, beside the gate.

## SCENE II.

A Muffled Figure. — LUIS and PAUL.

PAUL. There's no need to watch, for hither
Some one comes.

LUIS. A lucky mortal
Am I, if the hour draws nigh
That will two revenges offer.
 Since this night there then will be
Naught to interrupt my project,
Slaying first this muffled figure
And then Philip. Slow and solemn
Comes this man again. I know him
By his gait. But whence this horror
That comes o'er me as I see him,
This strange awe that chills, that shocks me?

THE FIGURE. Luis Enius!

LUIS. Sir, I've seen you
Here the last two nights; your object?
If you call me, wherefore fly thus?
If 'tis me you seek, why mock me

By retiring?

THE FIGURE. Follow me,
Then you'll know my name.

LUIS. I'm stopped here
In this street by a little business. —
To be quite alone imports me. —
Wherefore first by killing you
I'll be free to kill another
(He draws his sword, but merely cuts the air.
Draw, then, draw your sword or not,
Thus the needful path I shorten
To two acts of vengeance. Heavens!
I but strike the air, cut nothing,
Sever nothing else. Quick! Paul,
Stop him as he stalks off yonder,
Near to you.

PAUL. I'm bad at stopping.

LUIS. Then your footsteps I will follow
Everywhere, until I learn
Who you are. (Aside.) (In vain his body
Do I strive to pierce. Oh, heavens!
Lightnings flash from off my sword here;
But in no way can I touch him,
As if sword and arm were shortened.)
(Exit following the figure, striking at it without touching it.

### SCENE III.

PHILIP. — PAUL.

PAUL (aside). God be with you both! But scarce
Has one vanished, when another

Comes to haunt me. Why, I'm tempted
By strange phantoms and hobgoblins
Like another San Antonio: —
In this doorway I'll ensconce me,
Till my friend here kindly passes.

PHILIP. Love, ambitious, bold, deep-plotted,
With the favours of a kingdom
Me thou mak'st a prosperous lover.
To the desert fled Polonia,
Where, mid savage rocks and forests,
Citizen of mighty mountains,
Islander of lonely grottoes,
She doth dwell, to Lesbia leaving
Crown and kingdom; through a stronger
Greed than love I Lesbia court, —
For a queen is worth my homage.
From her trellis I have come,
From a sweet and pleasant converse.
But, what's this? Each night I stumble
On a man here at my doorstep.
Who is there?

PAUL (aside). To me he's coming.
Why on earth should every goblin
Pounce on me?

PHILIP. Sir, Caballero.

PAUL. These are names I don't acknowledge;
He can't speak to ME.

PHILIP. This house
Is my home.

PAUL. Which I don't covet;

May you for an age enjoy it,
Without billets.

PHILIP. If important
Business in this street detains you
(Not a word whereon I offer),
Give me room that I may pass.

PAUL (aside). Somewhat timid, though quite proper,
Goblins can be cowards too. —
Yes, sir, for a certain office
I am here; go in, and welcome;
I no gentleman would stop here
Bound for bed, nor is it right.

PHILIP. The condition I acknowledge. —
(Aside.
Well, fine spectres, to be sure,
Haunt this street: each night I notice
That a man here comes before me,
But when I approach him softly,
Hereabouts on my own threshold,
I, as now, have always lost him.
But what matters this to me?
(Exit.

(PAUL draws his sword and makes several flourishes.
PAUL. As he's gone, the right and proper
Thing is this: — Stay, stay, cold shadow,
Whether you're a ghost or ghostess,
I can't reach it. Why, by heaven!
Air alone I cut and chop here.
But if this is he we wait for
In the night-time like two blockheads
Faith! he is a lucky fellow
To have got to bed so promptly.

But another noise I hear
Sounding from that dark street yonder.
'Tis of swords and angry voices: —
There I run to reconnoitre.
(Exit.

## SCENE IV.

ANOTHER STREET.

The Muffled Figure and LUIS.

LUIS. Sir, already we have issued
From that street; if aught there stopped us,
We are here alone, and may
Hand to hand resume the combat.
And since powerless is my sword
Thee to wound, I throw me on thee
To know who thou art. Declare,
Art thou demon, man, or monster?
What! no answer? Then I thus
Dare myself to solve the problem,
(He tears the cloak from the Figure, and finds beneath it a skeleton.
And find out . . . . Oh, save me, heaven!
God! what's this I see? what horrid
Spectacle! What frightful vision!
What death-threatening fearful portent!
Stiff and stony corse, who art thou?
That of dust and ashes formed
Now dost live?

THE FIGURE. Not know thyself?
This is thy most faithful portrait;
I, alas! am Luis Enius.
(Disappears

LUIS. Save me, heaven! what words of horror!
Save me, heaven! what sight of woe!
Prey of shadows and misfortunes.
Ah, I die.
(He falls on the ground.

SCENE V.

PAUL. — LUIS.

PAUL. It is the voice
Of my master. Succour cometh
Opportunely now in me.
Sir!

LUIS. Ah! why return, dread monster?
I am overwhelmed, I faint here
At your voice.

PAUL (aside). God help his noddle!
He's gone mad! — Dread monster? No,
(Aloud.
I am Juan Paul, that donkey
Who, not knowing why or wherefore,
Is your servant.

LUIS. Ah! good, honest
Paul, I knew you not, so frightened
Am I. But at that why wonder,
If myself I do not know?
Did you see a fearful corse here,
A dead body with a soul,
An apparent man supported
By his skeleton alone,
Bones from which the flesh had rotted,

Fingers rigid, gaunt, and cold,
Naked trunk, uncouth, abhorrent,
Vacant spaces whence the eyes,
Having fallen, left bare the sockets? —
Whither has he gone?

PAUL. If I
Saw that ghost, upon my honour,
I could never say I saw it;
For more dead than that dead body
I had fallen on the other side
At the moment.

LUIS. And no wonder;
For my voice was mute, my breath
Choked, my heart's warm beat forgotten,
Clothed with ice were all my senses,
Shod with lead my feet, my forehead
Cold with sweat, I saw suspended
Heaven's two mighty poles upon me,
The brief Atlases sustaining
Such a burden being my shoulders.
It appeared as if there started
Rocks from every tender blossom,
Giants from each opening rose;
For the earth's disrupted hollows
Wished from out their graves to cast
Forth the dead who lay there rotten;
Ah, among them I beheld
Luis Enius! Heaven be softened!
Hide me, hide me, from myself!
Bury me in some deep corner
Of earth's centre! Let me never
See myself, since no self-knowledge
Have I had! But now I have it;
Now I know I am that monster

Of rebellion, who defied,
In my madness, pride, and folly,
God Himself; the same, whose crimes
Are so numerous and so horrid,
That it were slight punishment,
If the whole wrath of the Godhead
Was outpoured on me, and whilst
God was God, eternal torments
I should have to bear in hell.
But I have this further knowledge,
They were done against a God
So divine, that He has promised
To grant pardon, if my sins
I with penitent tears acknowledge.
Such I shed; and, Lord, to prove
That to-day to be another
I begin, being born anew,
To Thy hands my soul I offer.
Not as a strict judge then judge me,
For the attributes of the Godhead
Are His justice and His mercy;
With the latter, not the former,
Judge me, then, and fix what penance
I shall do to gain that object.
What will be the satisfaction
Of my life?

(Music (within). The Purgatory.

LUIS. Bless me, heaven! what's this I hear?
A sweet strain divine and solemn;
It appears a revelation
From on high, since heaven doth often
Help mysteriously the sinner.
And since I herein acknowledge
A divine interposition,

I will go into the Purgatory,
Called, of Patrick, and fulfil,
Humbly, faithfully, the promise
Which I gave him long ago,
If it is my happy fortune
To see Patrick. If the attempt
Is, as rumour hath informed me,
Most terrific, since no human
Strength avails against the horrors
Of the place, or resolution
To endure the demons' torments,
Still my sins I must remember
Were as dreadful. Skilful doctors
Give for dangerous diseases
Dangerous remedies to stop them. —
Come, then, with me, Paul, and see
How here penitent and prostrate
At the bishop's feet I'll kneel,
And confess, for greater wonder,
All my awful sins aloud.

PAUL. Go alone, then, for that project,
Since so brave a man as you are
Has no need of an accomplice;
And there's no one I have heard of
Who e'er went to hell escorted
By his servant. I'll go home,
And live pleasantly in my cottage
Without care. If ghosts there be,
I'm content with matrimony.
(Exit.

LUIS. Public were my sins, and so
Public penance I will offer
In atonement. Like one crazed,
Crying in the crowded cross-ways,

I'll confess aloud my crimes.
Men, wild beasts, rude mountains, forests,
Globes celestial, flinty rocks,
Tender plants, dry elms, thick coppice,
Know that I am Luis Enius,
Tremble at my name, that monster
Once of pride, as now I am
Of humility the wonder.
I have faith and certain hope
Of great happiness before me,
If in God's great name shall Patrick
Aid me in the Purgatory.
(Exit.

## SCENE VI.

A WOOD, IN THE CENTRE OF WHICH IS SEEN A MOUNTAIN, FROM WHICH POLONIA DESCENDS.

POLONIA.

POLONIA. To Thee, O Lord, my spirit climbs,
To Thee from every lonely hill
I burn to sacrifice my will
A thousand and a thousand times.
And such my boundless love to Thee
I wish each will of mine a living soul could be.

Would that my love I could have shown,
By leaving for Thy sake, instead
Of that poor crown that press'd my head,
Some proud, imperial crown and throne —
Some empire which the sun surveys
Through all its daily course and gilds with constant rays.

This lowly grot, 'neath rocks uphurled,

In which I dwell, though poor and small,
A spur of that stupendous wall,
The eighth great wonder of the world,
Doth in its little space excel
The grandest palace where a king doth dwell.

Far better on some natural lawn
To see the morn its gems bestrew,
Or watch it weeping pearls of dew
Within the white arms of the dawn;
Or view, before the sun, the stars
Drive o'er the brightening plain their swiftly-fading cars.

Far better in the mighty main,
As night comes on, and clouds grow grey,
To see the golden coach of day
Drive down amid the waves of Spain.
But be it dark, or be it bright,
O Lord! I praise Thy name by day and night.

Than to endure the inner strife,
The specious glare, but real weight
Of pomp, and power, and pride, and state,
And all the vanities of life;
How would we shudder could we deem
That life itself, in truth, is but a fleeting dream.

## SCENE VII.

LUIS. — POLONIA.

LUIS (aside). True to my purpose on I go,
With footsteps firm and bosom brave,
Seeking for that mysterious cave
Wherein the pitying heavens will show
How I salvation there may gain,

By bearing in this life the Purgatorial pain.
(To POLONIA.
Tell me, O holy woman! thou
Who in these wilds a home hast found,
A dweller in this mountain ground
Obedient to some sacred vow,
Which is the road to Patrick's cave,
Where penitential man his soul in life may save?

POLONIA. O, happy traveller! who here
Hast come so far in storm and shine,
Within this treasury divine
To feel and find salvation near,
Well can I guide thee on thy way,
Since 'tis for this alone amid these wilds I stray.

Seest thou this mountain?

LUIS. Ah! I see
My death in it.

POLONIA (aside). My heart grows cold.
Ah! who is this that I behold?

LUIS (aside). I cannot think it. Is it she?

POLONIA (aside). 'Tis Luis, now I know.

LUIS (aside). Perhaps illusion it may be
To baffle my intent, and lead
My erring feet astray. — (to POLONIA}. Proceed.

POLONIA (aside). Say, can it be to conquer me
The common enemy doth send
This spectre here?

LUIS. You do not speak.

POLONIA. Attend.
This mighty mountain, rock bestrown,
Full well the dreaded secret knows;
But no one to its centre goes
By any path o'er land alone:
He who would see this wondrous cave
Must in a bark put forth and tempt the lake's dark wave.

(Aside.) I struggle with a wish to wreak
Revenge, which pity doth subdue.

LUIS (aside). It doth my happiness renew
Once more to see and hear her speak.

POLONIA (aside). Within me opposite thoughts contend.

LUIS (aside). Ah, me! I die. — You do not speak.

POLONIA. Attend.
This darksome lake doth all surround
The lofty mountain's rugged base,
And so to reach the awful place
An easy passage may be found:
A sacred convent in the island stands,
Midway between the mountain and the sands.

Some pious priests inhabit there,
And for this task alone they live,
With loving zeal to freely give
The helping hand, the strengthening prayer —
Confession, and the Holy Mass,
And every needful help to all who thither pass.

Telling them what they first must do,

Before they dare presume to go,
Alive, within the realm of woe. —
(Aside.) Let not this enemy subdue
My soul, O Lord!

LUIS (aside). My hopes are fair.
Let me not feel, O Lord! the anguish of despair,

Seeing before my startled sight
My greatest, deepest crime arise;
Let not the fiend my soul that tries,
Subdue me in this dreadful fight.

POLONIA (aside). 'Gainst what a powerful foe must I defend
Myself to-day!

LUIS. You do not speak.

POLONIA. Attend.

LUIS. With quicker speed your story tell,
For well I know my soul hath need
That I should go with swifter speed!

POLONIA. And me it doth import as well
That you should go away.

LUIS. Agreed.
Now, woman, point the way to where my path doth lead.

POLONIA. No one accompanied can brave
The terrors of this gloomy lake;
And so a skiff you needs must take,
And try alone the icy wave;
Being in that most trying strait
The absolute master of your acts and fate.

Come where within a secret cave
Beside the shore the boat doth lie,
And trusting in the Lord on high,
Embark upon the crystal wave
Of this remote lone inland sea.

LUIS. My life and all I have I place, O Lord! in Thee.
And so I trust me to the bark;
But, O my soul! what sight is here,
A coffin doth the bark appear;
And I upon the waters dark
Alone must cross the icy tide.
(He enters.

POLONIA. Oh! turn not back, but follow and confide

LUIS (within). I've conquered! sweet Polonia's shade,
Since sight of thee has not undone
My shuddering soul.

POLONIA. And I have won,
Here in this Babylon delayed,
O'er wrath and rage the victory.

LUIS (within). Thy feigned resemblance does not frighten me,
Though thou dost take a form
Might tempt my steps astray
And make me turn despairing from my way.

POLONIA. Thy fear doth badly thee inform,
Poor to be brave and rich to be afraid,
For I Polonia am, and not her shade,
The same that thou didst slay,
But who by God's decree
Restored to life, even in this misery,

Is happier far to-day.

LUIS (within). Since I my sinful state
Confess, and feel too well its fearful weight,
Thy wrong, oh, pardon too!

POLONIA. I give it, and approve of thy design.

LUIS (within). My faith, at least, I never will resign.

POLONIA. That grace will be thy safeguard.

LUIS (within). Then, adieu!

POLONIA. Adieu!

LUIS (within). May God in pity save.

POLONIA. And bring thee back victorious from the cave.

## SCENE VIII.

THE ENTRANCE OF A CONVENT — AT THE END THE CAVE OF PATRICK.

Two Canons Regular; afterwards Luis.

FIRST CANON. See, the waters of the lake
Move although no breeze doth blow:
Without doubt to-day some pilgrim
Roweth to this island shore.

SECOND CANON. Come unto the strand to see
Who can be so brave and bold
As to seek our gloomy dwelling,
Crossing the dark waters o'er.

(Enter LUIS.

LUIS. Here my boat, my coffin, rather,
On the billows I bestow.
Who his sepulchre has ever
Steered, as I, through fire and snow?
What a pleasant spot is this!
Here has Spring, methinks, invoked
Flowers of high and low degree
To assemble at her court.
But this dismal mountain here,
How unlike the plain below!
Yet they are the better friends
By the contrasts that they show.
there the mournful birds of prey
Hoarsely croak, presaging woe,
Here the warblers in their joy
Charm us with their tuneful notes.
There the torrents leaping headlong
Fright us with their frenzied roar,
Here the crystal streamlets gliding
Mirror back the sun's bright gold.
Half way 'twixt that ugliness
And this beauty, I behold
A plain building whose grave front
Fear and love at once provokes.

FIRST CANON. Happy wanderer, who here
Hast arrived with heart so bold,
Come unto my arms.

LUIS. The ground
That you tread on suits me more.
Oh, for charity conduct me
To the Prior of your fold,
To the Abbot of this convent.

FIRST CANON. Though unworthy, you behold
Him in me. Speak. What's your wish?

LUIS. Father, if my name I told,
I'm afraid that swiftly flying,
With a terror uncontrolled,
You would leave me: for my works
Are so shocking to unfold,
That to see them not, the sun
Wraps him round in mourning robes.
I am an abyss of crimes,
A wild sea that has no shore;
I am a broad map of guilt,
And the greatest sinner known.
Yes, in me, to tell it briefly
In one comprehensive word
(Here my breath doth almost fail me),
Luis Enius behold!
I come here this cave to enter,
If for sins so manifold
Aught can ever satisfy,
Let my penance thus atone
To the Bishop of Hibernia
I've confessed, and am absolved,
Who informed of my intention
With a gracious love consoled
All my fears, and unto thee
Sent these letters I unfold.

FIRST CANON. Do not in a single day
Take, my son, a step so bold,
For these things require precaution
More than can at once be told.
Stay here as our guest some days,
Then at leisure we can both

See about it and decide.

LUIS. No, my father, no, oh, no!
Never from the ground I'll rise,
Where here prostrate I am thrown,
Till you grant to me this good.
It was God that touched my soul,
And inspired me to come here;
Not a vain desire to know,
Not ambition to find out
Secrets God, perchance, withholds.
Do not baffle this intention,
For the call is heaven's alone.
Oh, my father! yield in pity,
With me in my griefs condole,
Give my sorrows consolation,
Heal the anguish of my soul.

FIRST CANON. Luis, you have not considered
what you ask of me; you know
Nothing of the infernal torments
You must bear: to undergo
These your strength is insufficient.
Many are there, more the woe!
Who go in, but few, alas!
Who return.

LUIS. Your threats forebode
Much; but still they fright not me;
For I do protest, I go
But to purge away my sins,
Which if numbered are much more
Than the atoms of the sun
And the sands upon the shore.
I will ever have my hope
Firmly fixed upon the Lord,

At whose holy name even hell
Is subdued.

FIRST CANON. The fervid glow
Of your words compels me now
To unlock the awful doors.
Luis, you behold the cave:
See!
(He opens the mouth of the cave.

LUIS. Oh, save me, gracious God!

FIRST CANON. What! dismayed?

LUIS. No, not dismayed;
Still it scared me to behold.

FIRST CANON. I admonish you again,
For no lesser cause to go,
Than a firm belief that there
For your sins you may atone.

LUIS. Father, I am in the cave:
Listen to my voice once more,
Men and wild beasts, skies and mountains,
Day and night, and sun and moon,
To you all I here protest,
Ay, a thousand times make known,
That I enter here to suffer
Torments for my sins untold;
For so great, so dread a penance
Is but little to atone
For such sins as mine, believing
That the cave salvation holds.

FIRST CANON. Enter then, and in your mouth,

As within your heart's deep core,
Be the name of Jesus.

LUIS. Be
With me, Lord, O gracious Lord,
For here, armed but with Thy faith,
I am pitted 'gainst my foe
In the open field. That name
Will my enemy o'erthrow.
Crossing myself many times
I advance. Oh, save me, God!
(He enters the cave which they close.

FIRST CANON. Of the many who have entered
None has equal courage shown.
Oh, enable him, just Jesus,
To resist the demon host
And their wiles, relying ever
Upon Thee, divinest Lord.
(Exeunt.

## SCENE IX.

LESBIA, PHILIP, LEOGAIRE, The Captain, and POLONIA.

LESBIA. Before we reach the place,
Whither you wish to lead us, for a space
Let us say why we came
To see you here to-day: a definite aim
All of us here has brought.

POLONIA. Speak as we go whatever be your thought,
Still following where I lead,
For I a sight that doth all sights exceed
Will bring you here to see.

LESBIA. What, then, our wishes were you hear from me.
Polonia, you desired
In this wild mountain waste to live retired,
Making of me the heir,
While living, of your kingdom. I would share
With you in turn my plans, however small,
And so I hither come to tell you all.
My will is in your hands;
I ask not counsel, sister, but commands.
A single woman scarce can ever be
Strong through advice, and of necessity
She must be married.

POLONIA. Yes; and if your choice
Has fallen on Philip I may well rejoice,
For then to me you'll owe
Both crown and husband.

PHILIP. May you live whilst glow
The sun's bright beams, that orb which dies at night,
And Phoenix of its rays is born with morning's light.

POLONIA. Then since you thus have gained
Your wish, ye two, now free and unconstrained,
Listen to what I tell,
And all who hear me listen too, as well.
With all the outward show
Of fervour came a man, whom we all know,
Seeking for Patrick's cave,
To enter there, and so his soul to save.
He entered it, and cometh forth today,
And 'tis because my terror and dismay
Are balanced by my wonder, that with me
I bring you to behold this holy prodigy.
I do not tell you who he is lest fear
Should so my heart make craven, that I ne'er

Could reach the end I sought: —
'Tis for this object that you here are brought.

LESBIA. It is but only right
That I should mingle terror with delight.

POLONIA. If strength from him hath fled,
And he extended in the cave lies dead,
At least 'twill show
His punishment; and if he comes, we'll know
The mystery that is here;
If safe he comes, who cometh forth, through fear
Perchance he may not speak,
But, flying men, some solitude may seek
To live and die alone.

LEOGAIRE. What mighty mysteries lie here unknown.

CAPTAIN. The time is opportune that we come here,
For the religious whom we see draw near,
All bathed in tears, now go
To the cave's mouth in solemn, silent row
To throw the gates aside.

## SCENE X.

The procession advances to the cave; the gates are opened by the Prior and his assistants. LUIS ENIUS comes forth, astonished. — THE SAME.

PRIOR. And those of heaven, O Lord, keep open wide
To penitent tears and sighs.
May this poor sinner from these dungeons rise,
This dark and dismal place,
Where never shines the radiance of Thy face.

POLONIA. The gate is opened.

PRIOR. Oh, what happiness!

PHILIP. 'Tis Luis!

LUIS. Bless me, heaven! in pity bless!
Ah! is it possible that I am here
Again on earth after so many a year,
And that once more I see
The light of the sun?

CAPTAIN. How rapt!

LEOGAIRE. How dazed is he!

PRIOR. Embrace us all, my son.

LUIS. My arms were prison chains to every one.
Polonia, since thou'rt here,
Thy pity I may claim without a fear.
And thou, O Philip, know
That thrice an angel saved thee from the blow
Of my sharp sword: two nights I watched for thee
To slay thee; may my error pardoned be.
Now flying from myself, oh, let me hide,
And in some wilderness abide —
Far from the world in solitude and pain,
For he who saw what I have seen would feign,
So suffering live, so die.

PRIOR. Then on the part of God, O Enius! I
Command thee what thou hast seen at once to say.

LUIS. So sacred a command I must obey: —

And that the startled world may now begin
A better course, and man from mortal sin
My words may waken like some midnight wail,
Listen, O grave assembly to my tale.
After all the preparations,
Fit and solemn were effected,
Which in such a perilous case
Might be needed and expected,
And when I from all around me,
Firm in faith, with courage strengthened,
Tenderly farewell had taken
This dark cavern here to enter,
I my trust reposed in God,
And my lips repeating ever
Those mysterious, mystic words,
At which even the demons tremble,
I then placed me on the threshold,
Where, until, as I expected,
They would close the gate, I stood.
It was closed, and I remember
Then I found me in black night,
Whence the light was so ejected,
That I closed on it mine eyes.
(A strange way it seems, but certain
To see better in the dark.)
With my lids thus closed together
On I went, and felt a wall
Which in front of me extended;
And by following it, and groping
For about the length of twenty
Paces, came upon some rocks,
And perceived through a small crevice
Of this rugged mountain wall
That a doubtful glimmer entered
Of a light that was not light,
As when the day the dark disperses,

If 'tis morning, or not morning,
Oft the twilight is uncertain.
With light steps a path pursuing,
By the left-hand side I entered,
When I felt a strange commotion;
The firm earth began to tremble,
And upheaving 'neath my feet,
Ruin and convulsion threatened.
Stupified I stopped there, when
With a voice which woke my senses
From forgetfulness and fainting,
Loud a thunder-clap re-echoed,
And the ground on which I stood
Bursting open in the centre,
It appeared as if I fell
To a depth where I lay buried
In the loosened stones and earth
Which had after me descended.
Then I found me in a hall
Built of jasper, where the presence
Of the chisel was made known
By its ornate architecture.
Through a door of bronze twelve men
Then advanced and came directly
Where I stood, who, clothed alike
In unspotted snow-white dresses,
With a courteous air received me,
And too humbly did me reverence.
One, who seemed to be among them
The superior, said: "Remember
That in God you place your faith,
And that you be not dejected
In your battle with the demons;
For if moved by what they threaten,
Or may promise, you turn back,
You will have to dwell for ever

In the lowest depths of hell
Amid torments most excessive."
Angels were these men for me,
And so greatly was I strengthened
By their counsel and advice
That revived I once more felt me.
On a sudden then the whole
Hall unto mine eyes presented
Nothing but infernal visions,
Fallen angels, the first rebels,
And in forms so horrible,
So disgusting, that resemblance
It would be in vain to look for;
And one said to me: "Demented
Reckless fool, who here hast wished
Prematurely to present thee
To thy destined punishment,
And the pains that thou deservest;
If thy sins are so immense,
That thyself must needs condemn them,
Since thou in the eye of God
Never can have hope of mercy,
Why has thou come here thyself
To endure them? Back to earth, then,
Go, oh! go, and end thy life;
And as thou hast lived, so perish.
Then again thou'lt come to see us;
For hath hell prepared already
That dread seat in which thou must
Sit for ever and for ever." —
I did answer not a word;
And then giving me some heavy
Blows, my hands and feet they bound,
Tieing them with thongs together,
And then caught and wounded me
With sharp hooks of burning metal,

Dragging me through all the cloisters,
Where they lit a fire and left me
Headlong plunged amid the flames.
I but cried, "O Jesus! help me."
At the words the demons fled,
And the fire went out and ended
Then they brought me to a plain
Where the blackened earth presented
Fruits of thistles and of thorns,
'Stead of pink and rose sweet scented.
Here a biting wind passed by,
Which with subtle sharpness entered
Even my bones, whose faintest breath
Like the keenest sword-edge cleft me.
Here in the profoundest depths
Sadly, mournfully lamented
Myriad souls, their parents cursing
From whose loins they had descended.
Such despairing shrieks and cries,
Such blaspheming screams were blended,
Such atrocious oaths and curses
So repeated and incessant,
That the very demons shuddered.
I passed on, and in a meadow
Found me next, whose plants and grasses
Were all flames, which waved and bent them,
As when in the burning August
Wave the gold ears all together.
So immense it was, the sight
Never could make out where ended
This red field, and in it lay
An uncountable assemblage
All recumbent in the fire;
Through their bodies and their members
Burning spikes and nails were driven;
These with feet and hands extended

Were held nailed upon the ground,
Vipers of red fire the entrails
Gnawed of some; while others lying,
With their teeth in maniac frenzy
Bit the earth; and some there were
Piecemeal who themselves dismembered,
And who seemed to die, but only
To revive and die for ever.
There the ministers of death
Flung me from them bound and helpless,
But at the sweet name of Jesus
All their fury fled and left me.
I passed on, and found me where
Some were cured, by a strange method,
Of their cruel wounds and torments;
Lead and burning pitch were melted,
And being poured upon their sores
Made a cautery most dreadful.
Who that hears me will not mourn?
Who that hears this awful lesson
Will not sigh and will not weep,
Will not fear and will not tremble?
Then I saw a certain building,
Out of which bright rays extended
From the windows and the doors,
As when conflagration settles
On a house, the flame bursts forth
Where an opening is presented.
"This," they told me, "is the villa
Of delights, the bath of pleasures,
The abode of the luxurious,
Where are punished all those women
Who were in the other life,
From frivolity excessive,
Too much given to scented waters,
Unguents, rouges, baths, and perfumes." —

I went in, and there beheld,
In a tank of cold snow melted,
Many lovely women bathing,
With an upturned look of terror;
Underneath the water they
Were the prey of snakes and serpents,
For the fishes and the sirens
Of this sea they represented;
In the clear transparent crystal
Stiff and frozen were their members,
Icy hard their hair was lifted,
Chattering struck their teeth together.
Passing out, the demons brought me
To a mountain so tremendous
In its height, that as it rose
Through the sky its peak dissevered,
If it did not tear and rend,
The vast azure veil celestial;
In the middle of this peak
A volcano stood, which, belching
Flames, appeared as if to spit them
In the very face of heaven.
From this burning cone, this crater,
Fire at intervals ascended
In which issued many souls,
Who again its womb re-entered,
Oft repeating and renewing
This ascending and descending.
At this time a scorching wind
Caught me when I least expected,
Blowing me from where I stood,
So that instantly it set me
In the depths of that abyss.
I too was shot up: a second
Wind-gust came, that with it brought
Myriad legions, who impelled me

Rudely to another part,
Where it seemed I saw assembled
All the other souls I had seen,
But who here were all collected;
And though this was the abode
Where the pains were most excessive,
I remarked that all therein
Faces bore of glad expression,
Countenances calm and sweet,
No impatience in their gestures
Or their words; but with their eyes
Fixed on heaven, as if thus set there
To ask mercy, ever weeping
Tears of tenderness and penance.
That it was the Purgatory
I at once by this detected,
Where the happy souls are purged from
Their more venial offences.
I was not subdued even here,
Though the demons stormed and threatened
Me the more: I rather felt
By the sight renewed and strengthened.
Then they, seeing that they could not
Shake my constancy, presented
To my eyes their greatest torments,
That which is in an especial
Sense called hell; and so they brought me
To a river, all the herbage
Of whose banks was flowers of fire,
And whose stream was sulphur melted;
The dread monsters of its tide
Were the hydras and the serpents;
It was very wide, and o'er it
Was a narrow bridge suspended,
Which but seemed a line, no more,
And so delicate and slender

That in my opinion no one
Without breaking it could ever
Pass across. "Look here," they said,
"By this narrow way 'tis destined
Thou must cross; see thou the means.
And for thy o'erwhelming terror
See how those have fared who tried
Before thee." and then directly
I saw those who tried to pass
Fall into the stream, where serpents
Tore them in a thousand pieces
With their claws and teeth's sharp edges.
I invoked the name of God,
And could dare with it to venture
To the other side to pass,
Without yielding to the terror
Of the winds and of the waves,
Though they fearfully beset me.
Yes I passed, and in a wood,
So delightful and so fertile,
Found me, that in it I could,
After what had passed, refresh me.
On my way as I advanced,
Cedars, palms, their boughs extended,
Trees of paradise indeed,
As I may with strictness term them;
All the ground being covered over
With the rose and pink together
Formed a carpet, in whose hues
White and green and red were blended.
There the amorous song-birds sang
Tenderly their sweet distresses,
Keeping, with the thousand fountains
Of the streams, due time and measure.
Then upon my vision broke
A great city, proud and splendid,

Which had even the sun itself
For its towers' and turrets' endings;
All the gates were of pure gold,
Into which had been inserted
Exquisitely, diamonds, rubies,
Topaz, chrysolite, and emerald.
Ere I reached the gates they opened,
And the saints in long procession
Solemnly advanced to meet me,
Men and women, youths and elders,
Boys and girls and children came,
All so joyful and contented.
Then the seraphim and angels,
In a thousand choirs advancing,
To their golden instruments
Sang the symphonies of heaven;
After them at last approached
The most glorious and resplendent
Patrick, the great patriarch,
Who his gratulations telling
That I had fulfilled my word
Ere I died, as he expected,
He embraced me; all displaying
Joy and gladness in my welfare.
Thus encouraged he dismissed me,
Telling me no mortal ever,
While in life, that glorious city
Of the saints could hope to enter;
That once more unto the world
I should go my days to end there.
Finally my way retracing,
I came back, quite unmolested
By the dark infernal spirits,
And at last the gate of entrance
Having reached, you all came forward
To receive me and attend me.

And since I from so much danger
Have escaped, oh! deign to let me,
Pious fathers, here remain
Till my life is happily ended.
For with this the history closes,
As it is to us presented
By Dionysius the Carthusian,
With Henricus Salteriensis,
Matthew Paris, Ranulph Higden,
And Caesarius Heisterbacensis,
Marcus Marulus, Mombritius,
David Rothe, the prudent prelate,
And Vice-Primate of all Ireland,
Belarminus, Dimas Serpi,
Bede, Jacobus, and Solinus,
Messingham, and to express it
In a word, the Christian faith
And true piety that defend it.
For the play is ended where
Its applause, I hope, commences.

www.ingramcontent.com/pod-product-compliance
Lightning Source LLC
Chambersburg PA
CBHW050125170426
43197CB00011B/1724